# THE MODERN MERCENARY

# THE MODERN MERCENARY

## DOG OF WAR, OR SOLDIER OF HONOUR?

## Peter Tickler

**Patrick Stephens**
Wellingborough, Northamptonshire

First published in 1987

*British Library Cataloguing in Publication Data*

Tickler, Peter
The modern mercenary.
1. Mercenary troops
I. Title
355.3'5  EM  D848

ISBN 0-85059-812-5

Picture research: Military Archive and Research Services

*Patrick Stephens Limited is part of the
Thorsons Publishing Group*

Printed in Great Britain

1  3  5  7  9  10  8  6  4  2

# Contents

# Dedication

For Fiona, and in memoriam G. Richardson

# Acknowledgements

I have accumulated a number of debts in writing his book. Several of those who have assisted me prefer to remain anonymous, but I would like to record my thanks to Colin Evans in particular for his remarkable account of his time in Angola. Geoff Richardson was generous with his time despite suffering severely from a cancer which, sadly, finally defeated him. Victoria Schofield dug out some very interesting information for me. And Fiona Tickler exercised great patience, not least in preparing meals that were then uneaten! Though the subject is inappropriate, this book is dedicated to her.

# Sources

The material from which this book has been written derives from a number of different sources. These include interviews, correspondence and conversations with a number of individuals (anonymous and otherwise), press reports, television interviews, *Soldier of Fortune* magazine and a number of books, as listed below.

Banks, John, *The Wages of War: the Life of a Modern Mercenary*, London, 1978.

Burchett, Wilfred, and Derek Roebuck, *The Whores of the Wars: Mercenaries Today*, Harmondsworth, 1977.

Dempster, Chris, and Dave Tomkins, *Fire Power*, London 1978.

Halliday, Fred, *Mercenaries: 'Counter Insurgency' in the Gulf*, London, 1977.

Hoare, Mike, *Congo Mercenary*, London, 1967.

Mockler, Anthony, *The New Mercenaries*, London, 1985.

Report of the Committee of Privy Councillors appointed to enquire into the recruitment of mercenaries, London, 1976.

Seale, Patrick, and Maureen McConville, *The Hilton Assignment*, London, 1973.

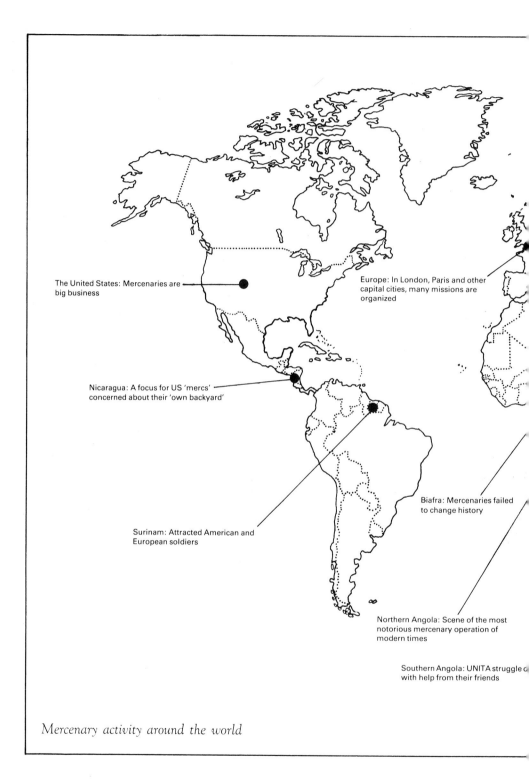

The United States: Mercenaries are big business

Europe: In London, Paris and other capital cities, many missions are organized

Nicaragua: A focus for US 'mercs' concerned about their 'own backyard'

Biafra: Mercenaries failed to change history

Surinam: Attracted American and European soldiers

Northern Angola: Scene of the most notorious mercenary operation of modern times

Southern Angola: UNITA struggle with help from their friends

*Mercenary activity around the world*

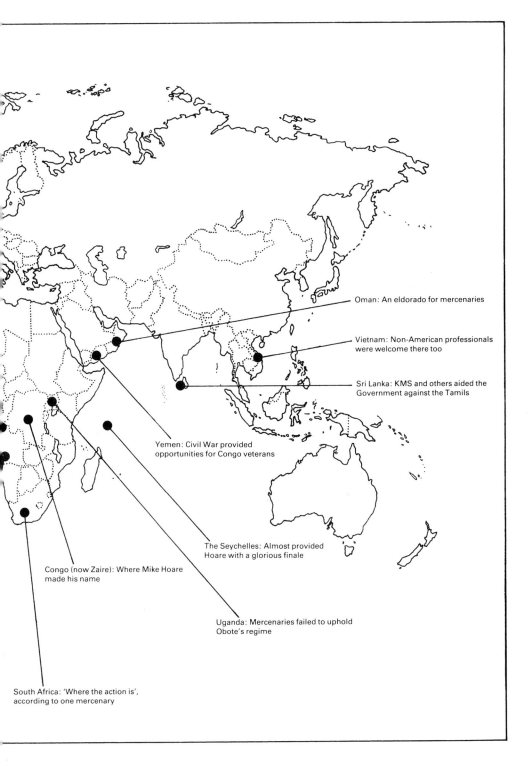

Oman: An eldorado for mercenaries

Vietnam: Non-American professionals were welcome there too

Sri Lanka: KMS and others aided the Government against the Tamils

Yemen: Civil War provided opportunities for Congo veterans

The Seychelles: Almost provided Hoare with a glorious finale

Congo (now Zaire): Where Mike Hoare made his name

Uganda: Mercenaries failed to uphold Obote's regime

South Africa: 'Where the action is', according to one mercenary

# Introduction

There have been mercenaries for as far back as history allows us to trace. In 401 BC 10,000 of them were hired by the pretender Cyrus as he strove to win the throne of the Persian empire. The attempt failed, but the mercenaries survived defeat and the death of Cyrus to retreat back through Asia Minor in a march recorded for posterity by Xenophon. His *Anabasis* makes exciting reading even today. Indeed it is not just the earliest example of the memoirs of a mercenary, but a classic account of a mercenary venture—and if there are times when the reader cannot help thinking that Xenophon's imagination is running away with him a bit, then the same can be said about many more recent writers. In this respect too, he has set standards by which other mercenary memoirs may be judged!

If mercenarism is not quite the oldest profession—though some might argue that it is a peculiarly male version of prostitution—it has effectively been around for as long as war has been waged. And far from dying out in the twentieth century, it has if anything enjoyed something of a revival in the last thirty years. The recent history of Africa contains many examples of mercenary activity, most notably in the Congo, Biafra and Angola, where the exploits of men like 'Mad' Mike Hoare, Rolf Steiner and 'Callan' have attracted much media attention. Yet the real growth in the mercenary trade lies not in the Dark Continent but in the oil-rich Middle East where foreign soldiers have had—and continue to have—an important influence on the unfolding of events.

The first question which any book on the subject has to face, however, is a deceptively simple one: what is a mercenary? In the public imagination he is a freelance soldier of no fixed abode or loyalty, ruthless, undertaking short contracts for large amounts of money, the sort of men depicted, for instance, by the film *The Wild Geese*, which was itself inspired by the exploits of Mike Hoare. There are certainly men around who fit, roughly speaking, into this category, but there are many more who do not. The mercenary is a man who fights in the pay of a power that is not his own country. Such a definition covers the Foreign Légionnaire; the (usually) British soldier serving in the forces of the Sultan of Oman; the Americans who defy the laws of their country to fight with the Contras against the Sandinista government of

Nicaragua; and men like 'Mark', who lives in a delightful farmhouse in northern England with a wife and two children, yet who earns his money by disappearing abroad for varying lengths of time on different types of military job. There are individuals and organizations willing and able to provide men to train recruits and fight for any cause that isn't Communist. (But Communists receive 'advisers' from the USSR, Cuba and other such countries, of course.) There are in the USA mercenary 'schools' willing to put would-be mercenaries through rigorous training programmes—at a price, of course. And a look through *Soldier of Fortune* magazine reveals the American obsession with the 'merc' way of life.

So despite the hopes of President Neto of Angola that the show trial of mercenaries captured in Angola in February 1976 would help to stamp out mercenarism, despite the fact that in some western countries it is officially illegal to be a mercenary, and despite the protestations of politicians that such things really should not be allowed, the mercenary flourishes. Indeed all the evidence goes to show that governments secretly approve of mercenaries, and monitor and foster their activities just so long as it does not compromise the national interest. The covert use of mercenaries makes good sense in the amoral world of high politics. If things go wrong, they can be disowned. If things go right, then so much the better.

This book looks, then, at the role of the mercenary in the world of today and yesterday. It looks in detail at some of the most famous or notorious mercenary operations of modern times, and assesses how widespread mercenarism is. It looks too at the mercenaries themselves, and asks how they become mercenaries, why they do it, and what makes them tick. It contains also a case study of Colin Evans, one of the mercenaries who served in Angola, fought alongside the notorious 'Callan', was captured by the MPLA forces and put on trial, served a term of imprisonment, and, finally and suddenly, was released after some eight years of captivity. Evans details here for the first time what it was like to live through such a sequence of experiences.

And, finally, this book poses the question: will mercenaries always be with us? Or are they, like prostitutes, too useful ever to be banned?

*Chapter 1*

# The Congo

In July 1964 Mike Hoare flew into Leopoldville, the capital of the Congo, at the request of an old friend, Gerry Puren. Puren was a close associate of the new Prime Minister of the Congo, Moise Tshombe, and had summoned Hoare on his own initiative. The Congo was racked by a fast-moving and violent rebel movement, and Tshombe had been appointed Prime Minister with the task of crushing it. The Armée Nationale Congolese (ANC) was showing little sign of being able to stem the victorious advance of the rebels, and it was Puren's estimate that Tshombe would soon be forced to use white mercenaries if the tide of events was to be turned. Hoare in fact had to wait some time, kicking his heels in Leopoldville, before the summons came, but when finally he was whisked off with Puren to meet Tshombe, the Prime Minister lost no time in getting time to the point. The meeting was over in five minutes, and the two old friends left with orders to raise a mercenary force to combat the rebels; Puren was to be in charge of the air force, while Hoare was to be in charge of raising, training and leading a force of soldiers whose job was to change the course of Congolese history.

In the next eighteen months Hoare was to fulfil his brief in spectacularly successful fashion, and in the process transformed himself from a nonentity to a household name round the world. He was pilloried in some quarters, lauded to the skies in others, enormously respected by his men—and beloved by the gentlemen of the Press, to whom the exploits (and supposed exploits) of 'Mad Mike' Hoare were food and drink.

In 1960, when the Congo had joined the growing band of independent African states, the emergence of a white mercenary leader in Black Africa must have seemed inconceivable. The mercenary seemed to be a historical figure, a man of the past with no role to play in the future. But the lessons of history show that there will always be a role for the hired professional soldier wherever war is waged; and whatever blessings the spread of independence brought to Africa, these did not include everlasting peace.

Independence came to the vast tract of land that was the Congo (and is now Zaire) on 30 June 1960. Yet just twelve days later Tshombe proclaimed that the wealthy area of Katanga was breaking away from the Congo to form a separate, independent state of which he was the first president. He was

*Mike Hoare arrived in the Congo a nonentity, and left a household name* (Camera Press).

supported in his actions by the Belgians, who provided him with practical military support in the form of arms and soldiers, but before long it became generally known, via advertisements and word of mouth, that opportunities existed in the Katanga gendarmerie or army for men with the right background and experience.

When Katanga came under pressure from the rebellious Balubas in the north as well as the ANC supported by United Nations troops, Tshombe turned for further help to France. His hopes of official backing from that country ultimately came to nothing, but not before some twenty French officers had flown in—most of whom decided to stay on. These included a paratroop officer of the French Foreign Legion, Robert Faulques, and he, a veteran of the campaigns in the Far East, now became the centre of a band of ex-paratrooper mercenaries which now began to form in Katanga.

The French Foreign Legion was the last great permanent mercenary force, and its members had fought with heroic courage in the 1950s in Indo-China. The 1er Régiment Etrangère de Parachutistes had been effectively wiped out on two occasions, but on each occasion it had been re-formed. When it returned to Algeria, it was given the task of 'cleaning up' the city of Algiers, and it carried out orders with methods which were as effective as they were brutal. In due course, De Gaulle was elected the new President of France, and before long it became apparent that he intended to withdraw the Legion from Algeria, a policy which many légionnaires saw as a betrayal of all that they had fought for. As a consequence, in April 1962 a group of Generals took power in Algiers, proclaiming their insistence that Algeria should remain French, and threatening even to drop paratroopers on Paris if De Gaulle did not reverse his policy. The Generals' support came above all from the 1er REP, and also from the other paratroop regiments, but it soon became apparent that the great majority of French soldiers in Algeria were not on their side, and the movement collapsed. The 1er REP suffered the ultimate punishment, and was disbanded in perpetuity.

One consequence of this, and of the general crisis of morale which engulfed the other regiments of the Legion, was that there were, suddenly, a lot of ex-légionnaires out of a job and so, potentially, on the mercenary market. With Faulques and other old comrades already out in the Congo, it is no wonder that many, unwilling or unable to settle into the pattern of civilian life, decided to follow them. And there they also met up with a number of English-speaking mercenaries, including, albeit rather briefly, Hoare.

The first significant battle involving mercenaries took place in September 1961 at Elizabethville, where the forces of Katanga, led by a Frenchman called Michel de Clay, and supported by an air force (if that is not an overstatement) of three antiquated planes and a helicopter, defeated the supposedly much superior UN forces from Ireland and Sweden. In early December, however, all four aircraft were destroyed on the ground, and in

the following week UN planes softened up Elizabethville with bombing and strafing attacks, before the armour and infantry moved in and took control of the city—though they only achieved victory after ferocious street fighting in which Faulques' men were conspicuous by their bravery and resource against numerically much superior forces. After this defeat, Faulques soon left Katanga, but others stayed on, including one of the heroes of the defence of Elizabethville, Bob Denard, a former French marine. A year later, the politicians having tried, but failed to come to a compromise settlement, the UN forces moved in again in strength and overran Katanga. The mercenaries, whose numbers probably did not reach even three figures, withdrew to Angola, along with several thousand Katangese troops. And that, as far as the independent state of Katanga was concerned, was that.

As far as mercenary activity in the Congo was concerned, however, it was anything but the end, for 1964 saw the rapid spread throughout the country of the so-called Simba revolt. The Simbas' success was due above all to the inspiration of Pierre Mulele, their leader, who claimed to be able to render them invulnerable to bullets by baptizing them with a special water. In a country where witch doctors and superstition held sway, such methods were immensely successful, not merely in convincing the Simbas that they were invulnerable, but in convincing their enemies too. Consequently all too often the forces of the ANC failed to put up any serious resistance to the advance

**Left** *A military conference on 3 January 1963. Left to right: Brigadier Noronha, Commander of UN troops in Elizabethville, General Guebre, C-in-C of the UN forces, and Brigadier Guha. The collapse of Katanga before much superior troops was this time swift* (The Photo Source).

**Right** *Inside a Simba arms 'factory'* (Camera Press).

of Simba troops, and the war cry 'Mai Mulele' ('mai' means water) was enough to strike terror into their souls.

Within a few months, the situation had reached such a pitch of crisis that the unthinkable happened. Moise Tshombe, who had led the abortive breakaway of Katanga, was on 30 June appointed Prime Minister of the Congo. This extraordinary development was due to the belief that in the circumstances he was the only man with the stature to lead the Congo out of the jaws of defeat. In early August, however, Stanleyville fell to the Simbas, and they thereupon proclaimed the People's Republic of the Congo. And so, as the rest of the world lined up on one side or the other—the Western powers supporting Tshombe, the Communists and most of the Arab countries behind his rival, President Christophe Gbenye—Tshombe, as he had done as President of Katanga, resolved to prosecute his cause with white mercenaries.

## Operation Watch-Chain

As soon as he was asked by Tshombe to raise a mercenary army, Hoare despatched Alastair Wicks, a friend from Katanga days, to Johannesburg to organize recruiting. Soon after his arrival there, Wicks entrusted matters to the hands of an old Harrovian friend, Patrick O'Malley, and himself flew up to Salisbury to personally conduct a recruiting campaign there. They were

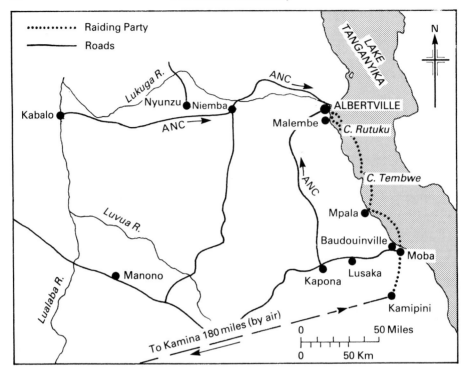

*Operation Watch-chain.*

given strict instructions to avoid publicity, but to hire large numbers of mercenaries in complete secrecy is virtually impossible, and before long both men had been featured in newspapers and on television. Embarrassing though this was to Hoare, it was nevertheless a remarkably effective way to attract recruits (John Banks was likewise to find the media extremely co-operative when he was recruiting for Angola). Within three weeks, Hoare was informed that a thousand recruits had signed up. The bandwagon was, it seemed, well and truly rolling.

Carried away by this news, Hoare decided that he must launch an immediate mercenary operation. He was determined to show the people of the Congo that the rebels could be defeated, and his mercenaries were the men to do it. He also hoped that his activity would goad the ANC into more positive and resolute action than they had so far demonstrated. The obvious place for a demonstration of mercenary power was the important town of Albertville, on the shore of Lake Tanganyika. It had fallen into the hands of the rebels, and the Belgian priests and civilians who had been captured there were reported to be in grave danger of being killed by the rebels. It was, therefore, imperative that the town be captured without delay. Although two ANC columns were already combining in a double thrust on the town, they were making slow progress. That under Colonel Kakuji, advancing from the west, had become bogged down at Kongolo, north of Kabalo, while the other battalion, under Lieutenant-Colonel Bangala, had ground to a halt on the road leading north from Kapona to Albertville.

Hoare reckoned this to be an ideal opportunity to show the mettle of his men and himself. He believed that he needed a force of just a hundred men to launch a successful amphibious operation which would both save the threatened Belgians and grab a slice of military glory for his own mercenary army. Since Albertville lay on the shore of Lake Tanganyika, Hoare determined that the best way to attck it was to advance by boat from the settlement of Moba in the south along the western edge of the lake. With the advantage of surprise and the controlled firepower of a hundred experienced men, he was convinced that he had every chance of achieving a dramatic change in the fortunes of the war.

It was a bold, imaginative plan, but from the very start it was dogged by misfortune. When Hoare went to reconnoitre Moba, he found the lakeside town had been completely devastated by the rebels; its buildings had been razed to the ground, its inhabitants were gone, and there was not a boat of any description to be found. Much more serious, however, was the setback which Hoare encountered when he went to Kamina airport to welcome the hundred mercenary recruits who were due to be flying in on two DC-4s. In the event, only one plane touched down, and even that was not full for only 38 men disembarked. Hoare, not surprisingly, felt misgivings, but was determined to carry on with the operation for reasons of morale, and he remained immovable in his plans even when, after he had outlined them to the new arrivals, nine promptly opted out on the grounds that they hadn't yet signed a contract. This was not, perhaps, so unreasonable in the circumstances but, as Hoare caustically commented, 'it came as a bit of a shock to many of them that this was a shooting war where a man could get himself killed'. But even the remaining 29 were hardly the hardened, experienced old soldiers whom Hoare had been expecting. When he got them drilling, he quickly assessed his material and concluded that only about a dozen of them were veterans. The most striking of them was a German, Siegfried Müller, who had won the Iron Cross in the Second World War and who proudly requested permission to wear it. Hoare agreed, though what impressed him most about Müller on this first meeting was not the medal so much as the fact that he had brought a typewriter with him—a true sign of an experienced soldier.

While his men were issued with equipment, familiarized themselves with their Spanish FN rifles, and prepared the assault boats, Hoare finalized the details of his plan. The very next day they would fly down to Kampini, and from there they would drive to Moba; they would embark on their boats by night, and two and a half days later they would attack and capture

Albertville airport. They would then hold the airport until reinforcements could be flown in, and after that help rescue the Belgians held prisoner in Albertville before they could be slaughtered.

That was the theory, but in practice things turned out very differently. Indeed, Hoare was immediately hit by a critical piece of misfortune—the non-arrival of his wireless sets. Although he knew that this was a body blow to his plans, he refused to call off the operation, and the next day the small force set off to Kampini and thence to Moba. But when Hoare himself arrived at the desolate lakeside settlement late that evening, he was greeted by Lieutenant Pat Kirton with news of yet more trouble. The men were in mutinous mood, and were refusing to go on the lake. The troublemaker was a Belgian who had been telling his comrades how rough the lake could get and warning them they would all end up drowning.

That was not all. One of the four assault boats had been damaged in transit, and Hoare, when he saw the hole in the hull, was convinced that it was a piece of deliberate sabotage, not a mere accident. Hoare called over the Belgian. He repeated his views on the lake and said that none of the men were prepared to risk it. It was a make or break situation for Hoare, and he responded to the challenge to his leadership by pulling out his pistol and with a single blow, knocking the mutineer to the ground. In the time which it took for his limp body to fall, all resistance to Hoare collapsed, but he nevertheless decided to leave six of the others behind, as well as the Belgian, judging that faint-hearted troops were of no use on such a mission. This left him with just 22 men and himself with which to carry out an operation which had been conceived with a force of 100 men in mind. By any standards, it was a gamble.

The small group embarked in the three sound boats shortly after midnight, and proceeded north until dawn. The following day, as they rested up, a motor boat came into view. It was piloted by a white priest, who carried the news that the sixty Belgian priests held in Albertville prison were due to be killed in the next 48 hours. He begged Hoare to forget his plans to take the airfield, but to aim directly for the gaol, and Hoare, against his better judgement, allowed himself to be persuaded, despite the fact that the capture of the airport—which would allow reinforcements to be flown in—was the very nub of his plan.

The night which followed saw no improvement in Hoare's fortunes. Two of the outboard motors broke down, all his men were forced to resort to paddles, and by the time they beached their craft at dawn, they were still some fifteen miles short of Albertville. Hoare forced his men to continue on foot, exhausted though they all were, and slowly they made their way to the village of Malenda where, at midday, they were at last allowed to stop, to swim, and to sleep. They were roused some time later by screaming villagers who warned them that a force of rebels was approaching fast. Hoare's men grabbed their rifles and fell in while he himself trained his binoculars for his first ever view of Simbas. At first he was puzzled by the way they advanced, swaying to and fro in a peculiar manner, and it was only as they drew closer that he realized why: they were high on the drug *dawa*. It was a tense moment for Hoare's unblooded men as the fearless Simbas jogged forward screaming 'Mai Mulele' at the tops of their voices, but they kept their nerves and held their fire until their attackers were at close range. Hoare fired the first shot, which heralded a frantic burst of largely inaccurate shooting, but a Dutch veteran, Van de Hoek, showed great composure in picking off his targets one by one, and before long it was all over Only three rebels escaped from the field of battle, leaving 28 of their comrades dead and dying, and Hoare's force had achieved its first victory—a terrific boost for morale even though the defeat of 31 men armed with a mixture of Mausers, pangas and knives hardly constituted a great military triumph.

When questioning of the locals revealed that the only route by foot to Albertville was via a circuitous road of some thirty kilometres, Hoare reverted to his original plan of attacking by water, and again he decided to concentrate his initial attack on the airfield. He commandeered two fishing boats to replace the engineless assault boats, but an attempt to land near Albertville by night ended in chaos, and they were forced to withdraw to Malembe and dig into a strong defensive position just south of the village.

There they stayed for two days, waiting for supplies to be dropped, but as these failed to materialize Hoare's impatience got the better of him and he decided to paddle all the way to the airfield, come what may. It took eleven hours to make it, but when they finally landed they did so undetected and without a shot being fired. They were astonished to find the airfield deserted, but before establishing themselves there they went to investigate a large lighted building a little way down the road. Eric Bridge, one of Hoare's Lieutenants and formerly a Marine, went forward to scout it out, but was spotted by a sentry who fired at him and raised the alarm. Simbas started to pour out of the building and the mercenaries, heavily outnumbered and having failed to take their foe by surprise, were forced to beat a fighting retreat to the beach. Bridge was badly wounded, and two Germans in Müller's section were killed, but the rest managed to embark with some difficulty. Their problems were not over, however. A strong wind arose which whipped up the lake until the boats were in danger of being swamped, and it took some fourteen hours of desperate paddling before they finally regained the safety of dry land near Malembe. After a night of exhausted sleep, they were then faced with two more days of paddling to reach the Mpala Mission where the priests gave them shelter, and Hoare gave thanks to God for getting most of them out alive. The next day the ANC battalion of Colonel Kakuji took Albertville, and managed to save most of the Belgians

who had been imprisoned there by the Simbas. The mercenary side of the operation had been a total failure. Almost everything that could have gone wrong did so, and Hoare's reputation had, as a consequence, reached rock bottom.

Not that Hoare was totally disillusioned by the experience. Indeed, he was delighted with the spirit displayed by those mercenaries who had seen the operation through. But spirit alone does not win wars, and he drew from the episode one crucial lesson: that training was the key to success in the Congo. He therefore resolved that all his future recruits should undergo a thorough basic training before being committed to battle.

Recruits were assembling in Kamina, a military base built by the Belgians, in some numbers, and when Hoare flew in to take charge of them he found no less than 500 awaiting him. They comprised nineteen different nationalities—though the majority, not surprisingly, were South Africans and Rhodesians—and were in other respects too a decidedly mixed bunch. Too mixed for Hoare's liking. Indeed he found the standard of recruits to be 'alarmingly low', and was surprised at the number of alcoholics, drug addicts, homosexuals, and 'bums and layabouts' who had come out to the Congo in search of what they thought would be easy money. His first task, then, was to set about a vigorous pruning, and before long he had reduced their numbers from 500 to 300.

**Left** *The graves of the two German mercenaries killed on the ill-fated amphibious expedition against Albertville* (The Photo Source).

**Right** *A white mercenary stares suspiciously at a dead Simba on the side of the road* (Popperfoto).

**Left** *Two of Mike Hoare's more experienced recruits; Vic Oglethorpe (left) had already fought for Tshombe in Katanga in 1960, while Dougie Lord, a former corporal in the British Army, had been awarded medals during the Second World War (Popperfoto).*

**Right** *Recruits sign on the dotted line. The contracts were comprehensive, but pay was always slow in coming through (Associated Press).*

The most common motive, he found, was the obvious one—the hope of making a sizeable amount of money. There were also a few idealists who saw themselves as crusaders against Communism, and there were a few adventurers, but these were in a minority. The pay was, in theory at least, good. Hoare had spent some time in negotiating terms, and the basic pay for a Private was £140 a week, of which at least half was to be paid in sterling. In addition, there were also various allowances, for a wife, for each legitimate child, for time spent in 'danger' and 'insecure' zones, and for board and lodgings. Also stipulated in the contract were compensation payments in the event of death or injury. In the case of death, there was a basic payment of one million Belgian francs, plus a further hundred thousand for each legitimate child whom the deceased left. Furthermore, the loss or loss of function of virtually any part of the body entitled the volunteer (as each mercenary was officially called) to a percentage payment—this ranged from 35 per cent for the right arm (or left arm if you were left handed!) to five per cent for the big toe and three percent for any of the other toes. The length of contract was six months, at the end of which the volunteer was entitled to twenty days' paid leave. Although it was hoped that many would sign up for a second spell of service after their first one, in practice few did. Also in practice pay was irregular, and on more than one occasion Hoare had to face complaints from his men on that score.

With the pruning complete, 'Mad Mike' set about turning his mercenaries into an efficient fighting force. His organization was very much along the lines of the British Army, and he was particularly strict on matters of personal appearance. The Belgians of Katanga had revelled in the nickname of Les Affreux, 'The Frightful Ones', a name deriving from their propensity not to shave for days at a time and to wear what they felt like. But this was something Hoare was not prepared to tolerate—both because he felt it reflected and encouraged a lack of discipline, and also because he was anxious that his mercenaries should appear in a much better light to the world at large. Thus he insisted that his men always shaved every day, and he had a horror of what he terms 'fancy dress'.

'I remember some of those blokes very well in Katanga in 1961 with their heavy beards, bandoliers, grenade stuck in the belt, rolled-down socks and invariably those shorts—the ones that were so short their balls were hanging out. That was my idea of hell. . . . The average mercenary loves dressing up. . . but it's not part of soldiering.'

Hoare put the 300 men who were to form 5 Commando through two months of punishing training. Physical fitness work and hour after hour on the firing range were the keynotes of his progress, though he also took care to conduct a number of sessions with his officers and NCOs on possible tactics. Since there was no book on the Congo, he said, they would have to write it themselves.

The plan was that after a sustained period of training, 5 Commando should form the spearhead of a Brigade whose first task would be to capture Kongolo and Stanleyville, but the pressure caused by the continuing Simba successes was such that Hoare found himself having to allow units of his men to be detached to meet threats elsewhere before they had received what he considered to be essential training. Indeed he had to let forty men, whom he designated 51 Commando, leave Kamina without having undergone any training at all. They were, nevertheless, spectacularly successful, recapturing with remarkable ease first Lisala, then Bumba. These victories showed the potential of white mercenaries in a much more favourable light than had Operation Watch-chain, and before long 52, 53, and 54 Commandos had

also been detached from the main body at Kamina. They too enjoyed considerable success, though this fragmentation of his forces irked Hoare who sought an interview with Tshombe to air his grievances. Tshombe was sympathetic, but was not prepared to interfere in military matters. However, Colonel Vanderwalle had no desire to see the strength of the central mercenary force dissipated any further either, and at the end of October 55, 56, and 57 Commandos moved from Kamini to Kongolo whence they were to play a key part in the planned advance on Stanleyville.

Indeed, Hoare's men, preceded by an armoured group of two Ferret scout cars and three Scania Vabi armoured cars, were to form the spearhead of the motorized column which now assembled at Kongolo. They were to be supported by a much larger force of ANC troops, but it was the mercenaries and the armour who would bear the brunt of any ambushes and would lead the attacks on defended positions. The whole of the column was under the command of another Belgian officer, Lieutenant-Colonel Liegois.

The advance on Stanleyville started well, as Samba, then Kibombo, fell without undue difficulty. But the first real test of nerve came when Liegois, anxious to reach Kindu before the enemy had a chance to regroup there, determined to press straight on from Kibombo without any respite. This entailed a night advance, and to achieve maximum speed Liegois ordered that headlights should be used. The mercenaries were far from happy about such tactics, which seemed to invite ambush, and before long their worst fears were fulfilled at a point where the road entered a deep cutting. As machine-guns spat tracer and bullets from out of the dark, jeeps and lorries emptied instantaneously as men dived for cover. When Hoare edged his way forward, he saw that three armoured cars were blocking their path, but the situation was soon rectified by the leader of 56 Commando, Captain Ian Gordon—'the nearest thing to a perfect fighting man that I was to meet in

**Left** *Mike Hoare in contemplative mood. Note the 5 Commando badge on his shoulder* (Camera Press).

**Right** *Mercenaries meeting resistance during their advance on Boende, whose capture in October was a prelude to the advance on Stanleyville* (Popperfoto).

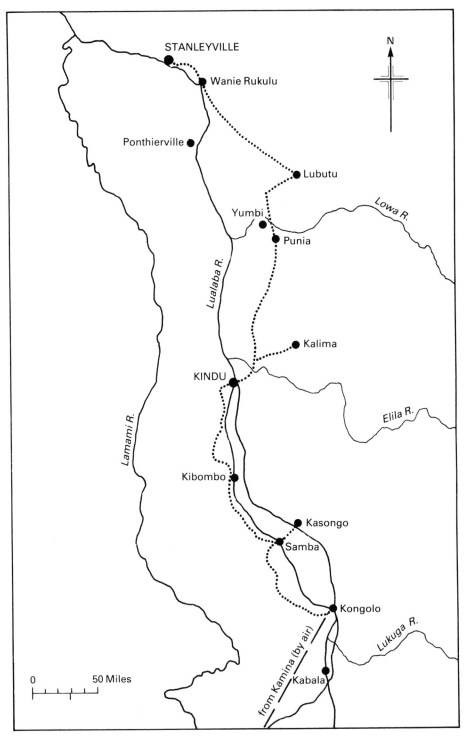

N

STANLEYVILLE

Wanie Rukulu

Ponthierville

Lubutu

Lowa R.

Yumbi

Punia

Lualaba R.

Kalima

KINDU

Elila R.

Lamami R.

Kibombo

Kasongo

Samba

Kongolo

Lukuga R.

from Kamina (by air)

Kabala

0          50 Miles

the Congo', as Hoare described him. Despite heavy fire, he moved forward with a bazooka and, with a single rocket, destroyed the nearest enemy armoured car. The spectacular explosion both lit up the whole scene and terrified the occupants of the other two armoured cars. They jumped out of their vehicles, but were cut down by machine-gun fire before they could reach cover.

The ambush, unsuccessful though it had been, caused Liegois to revise his tactics, and the column thereafter advanced with lights out and at just 10 mph until, at 03:00 hours, he ordered a halt and allowed them all three hours' sleep. Then they were off again. The speed of their advance took the enemy completely by surprise. At one point they drove into a village and came face to face with two buses of Simba warriors. Although most of them fled into the bush, one or two were taken prisoner, and interrogation revealed that they had no idea that the column had penetrated so far.

The actual attack on Kindu was typical of the tactics which were to be used time and again by 5 Commando—a softening up of the enemy with air attacks followed by high-speed attack by the mercenaries. In this case Alastair Wicks, who was liaising with the air force (which was piloted by anti-Castro Cubans!), asked them to pummel Kindu until the very last moment. They carried out these instructions to the letter. Indeed, as Hoare and his men raced nearer and nearer the town, and still the planes continued to rocket and machine-gun the defenders, he grew more and more anxious. 'Tell them to stop', he yelled at Wicks as some rocket shrapnel hurtled dangerously close. Then they were in the town, careering along with guns blazing. Moving at speed, their fire was inevitably inaccurate, but it mattered little since few

**Left** *The advance on Stanleyville.*

**Right** *Members of 5 Commando clear a house in Kindu during the advance on Stanleyville* (Popperfoto).

of the enemy showed any stomach for the fight. Many tried to escape by means of the ferry, but when its engine suddenly stopped, the unwieldy vessel became a death trap: as it floated slowly downstream, it was an easy target for some of the men of 57 Commando who, with the ruthless ex-SAS man, Sergeant John Peters, to the fore, systematically picked off their targets so that when it had finally drifted out of range, very few men were left alive on it.

The capture of Kindu did wonders for both the morale and standing of the men of 5 Commando. Not only was it an important victory achieved with relative ease, but it also led to the salvation of many Europeans. Grim stories had been circulating of the atrocities being visited on the Europeans held at Kindu, but in the event many were found safe and well. Indeed, the next few days saw the rescue of priests and civilians from a number of outlying settlements too. They also saw the death of one of Hoare's most reliable officers, ex-Coldstream Guardsman Jeremy Spencer; he was hit by a sniper while defending Elila bridge, just north of Kindu, against a counter-attack, and died instantly.

When Liegois ordered the advance to continue, the column swept forward with little delay or resistance until it reached the river Lowa. The Simbas had selected this natural barrier to be their next defensive position and were dug in on the far bank. An opposed river crossing was not something for Hoare's men to relish, but they had the invaluable backing, now as nearly always in the Congo, of an unchallenged air force, and this was a vital ingredient to their success. Thus 55 Commando, under the cover of air support, mortars, and heavy machine-gun fire, and led by Hoare's newly promoted Regimental Sergeant Major, Jack Carlton-Barber, stormed across the river and drove the

**Above left and above** *Jeeps mounted with machine guns were very typical forms of transport used by mercenaries under Hoare and subsequent commanders. They were well suited to the basic but usually effective tactics of driving flat out into defended towns with guns blazing. In such circumstances, the fire might not be accurate, but it tended to have the desired effect of panicking the defenders. Note the camouflage on the front of the Jeeps* (Rex Features).

enemy from their prepared positions without suffering a single casualty.

It was shortly after this, on 20 November, that Hoare received news of a startling development. A force of Belgian paratroopers had flown into Ascension Island, and was on stand-by for a drop over Stanleyville. In the last few weeks, every European whom the adherents of the Popular Republic of the Congo could lay their hands on had been rounded up: some 300 were held in Stanleyville itself, and many others in settlements throughout the surrounding region. They had immediately become pawns in a deadly game of blackmail, with Christophe Gbenye threatening to kill them all in a desperate attempt to gain a respite for his suddenly beleaguered movement, but far from buying him time this wild threat merely provoked the Belgian government into taking unilateral action and flying in their paratroopers.

Yet despite the imminent risk of a letting of European blood in Stanleyville and elsewhere, no orders were given for the column to advance. For three whole days Hoare agonized and fumed at the delay, convinced that an immediate advance on Stanleyville was the best course open—it would maximize the element of surprise, and give them the best possible chance of reaching 'Stan' before it was too late. Hoare talked it over long and hard with his confidant and No 2 Wicks, but although at one point he firmly resolved

*Christophe Gbeyne, who used European hostages in Stanleyville in a desperate game of blackmail. Many were killed before Belgian paratroopers parachuted in and took the city in advance of Hoare's men (Camera Press).*

to ignore Liegois' orders and to advance with his men the following dawn, in the end his nerve failed him and he made no move.

They waited until the middle of the afternoon of 23 November when Colonel Vanderwalle suddenly flew in and, after urgent consultation, issued the orders to advance. The Belgian paratroopers, he revealed, were now based at Kamina and would jump over Stanleyville aerodrome the following morning at 06:00 hours, weather permitting. The column must therefore move out within the hour, at 16:00 hours, and be in a position to attack Stanleyville at the same time as the paratroopers were dropping from the sky. This would involve moving through hostile territory by night, something which filled Hoare with apprehension. After his earlier experiences of such tactics, he had firmly resolved never to employ them again in the Congo, but in the circumstances he had little choice even though it meant that the lights of the convoy would make it an easy target for ambush.

Hoare's fears were confirmed when, soon after nightfall, the first ambush hit the column. No casualties were sustained, but a little later a second ambush left one of the Cubans who made up the newly arrived 58

Commando seriously wounded. Further on, one of Hoare's Sergeants, Freddy Basson, was killed and two other men wounded, and this was followed by the death of a news reporter, George Clay, hit by a burst of machine-gun fire even as he operated his tape recorder on what was scheduled to be his last assignment. This was too much for Hoare, who confronted Vanderwalle and told him that he would not allow his men to advance any further until daybreak. The Colonel agreed—as he had to—until dawn brought to an end what Hoare was later to describe as the 'most terrifying and harrowing experience of my life'.

This delay meant that they were unable to attack Stanleyville in concert with the paratroopers as had been the original plan. The paratroopers in fact dropped over Stanleyville aerodrome at 06:35 hours, and swiftly forced their way to the centre of the town, but not before the Simbas had assembled all the hostages in a group outside and, as the noise of the fighting became louder and closer, opened fire on their wretched prisoners. By the time the paratroopers reached the scene, 24 of them were dead, and another forty horribly wounded (five of whom were later to die). Colonel Vanderwalle's column arrived some time later, relieved that their nightmarish journey was over, appalled by the sight which greeted them, and with a sense of being cheated of a showdown with the Simbas.

They were not, however, too late to enjoy the 'fruits of victory'. Hoare had very strict orders against looting, but on this occasion he turned a blind eye to the rapacious activities of his men. He later defended his position by explaining that since the ANC soldiers were the first to start looting, and since his own men would be bound to be blamed for it anyway, they might as well join in. There was certainly some perverse logic in his thinking, but it smacks too of an apologia—and the reality was that Hoare would have had great difficulty in restraining his men even if he had tried to.

In such a situation, maintaining control over the mercenaries could hardly have been easy, and Hoare was that first night in Stanleyville faced with a difficult decision on which the credibility of his leadership depended. This occurred when he was woken by a deputation of his own officers (Hoare was later careful not to say which officers) who insisted that he hold an immediate trial of a mercenary on the charge of murder. They alleged that this man had raped a Congolese girl, then taken her down to the river and shot her dead. Hoare at first tried to duck the issue on the grounds that the man was not a member of 5 Commando, but they insisted that authority lay with him and that he must set an example which his own men might heed. Otherwise, they insisted, everyone in 5 Commando who was so minded would feel that he had a licence to rape and kill. Hoare reacted to this by saying that his men were not like that, whereupon they asked him, pointedly, how well he thought he knew his men. This question forced his reluctant hand. The hold which a mercenary leader has over his men is inevitably somewhat tenuous, and Hoare knew that if he did not act firmly now he was at real risk of losing control of 5 Commando altogether.

The accused man was immediately arrested and, that very night, tried by Hoare and his three fellow officers. He was found guilty—there was no doubt about that—but the problem was what punishment to mete out to him. Hoare told each of his fellow judges to write down their own suggestsions and then to hand him the pieces of paper. Hoare himself did so too, and then read out the proposed sentences. One suggested a 35-strike flogging; the other two proposed death—one a straightforward shooting, the other an enforced suicide. Hoare, however, was unwilling to execute a mercenary despite the callous brutality of his crime, and opted for a more bizarre punishment which, he hoped, would ensure the continued obedience and loyalty of his men—the removal of the man's big toes. The others agreed. The condemned man was dragged down to the river where he had committed the murder and, while he was pinned down by the three unnamed officers, Hoare shot off his big toes with two shots from his pistol. It was a brutal punishment—smacking more of the rule of the jungle than of impartial justice—and had been selected by Hoare because he knew the man was a professional footballer in his home country.

This may be compared with an incident which occurred on the march to Stanleyville only a short while before. 5 Commando had occupied the hill town of Lubutu without a shot being fired on 22 November. During the night of the 22nd/23rd a lone rebel truck drove into the town and up to the hospital. Its lights had been spotted by a sentry when it was still some way distant, but the mercenaries made no attempt to stop it since the driver was clearly under the misapprehension that Lubutu was still in rebel hands. When the truck stopped, an officer got out. A sentry immediately shot him dead. Several other men, who were apparently asleep in the back, leapt out; as they ran for the cover of the bush, four of them were also gunned down. One of Hoare's Lieutenants, a Belgian, went up and inspected the vehicle. He found, crouched in the back, another rebel—a boy of about eight. Documents which the mercenaries later found on the dead officer revealed that he was being taken to the hospital to receive treatment for a broken arm. Hoare's Lieutenant pulled him from the truck and shot him too.

Hoare, who had been warned of the approach of the truck when it was first spotted, thought nothing of it, and went back to sleep. It was only the next morning, when he inspected the scene of the incident, that he learnt exactly what had happened. According to his own account, he was furious at the killing of the boy, and became even more so when he learnt that the killer was none other than the Belgian mercenary who had caused him trouble at Moba on the shore of Lake Tanganyika some months previously. 'This time I fixed him forever.'

Hoare's behaviour is illuminating, not least because it was only the killing

of the boy which provoked his anger. The fact that the four men who had
also been killed were gunned down in cold blood—the rebels had been taken
totally unawares and made no attempt to fire their weapons—had no affect
on him. The killing of the boy—while certainly more culpable in that it was
even more wanton and cold-blooded—seems merely to have been an example
of such callous methods being taken to their logical extremes. If the former
is acceptable, and the latter not, where precisely does the dividing line lie?
The dividing line, Hoare might respond, is that of adulthood. The men were
soldiers, the boy was just a boy. But did Hoare, on the morning of the 23rd,
really draw such a distinction? As he himself documents, it was the young
rebels, the jeunesse, who were alleged to be some of the most brutal torturers
and killers of the captives; one of the defenders of Albertville had been a
twelve-year-old who had been promoted to Sergeant-Major as a result of his
remarkable brutality.

Hoare's 'execution' of his Lieutenant, although prompted by the
unnecessary killing of an eight-year-old, was motivated ultimately, it seems,
not by any pious sense of justice, but by a determination to deal with a man
whom Hoare saw as a troublemaker. The man had caused him much trouble
at Moba; this was an opportunity for Hoare to ensure that he didn't cause
him any more trouble in the future; so Hoare 'fixed him for good'. That is
to say, he shot him down out of hand without even resorting to a drumhead
courtmartial, just as the Belgian had shot down the boy. It was,
unquestionably, justice, if of a distinctly rough sort. But the whole incident
is interesting for the sharp light that it throws on mercenary behaviour in the
Congo. On the one hand it shows how brutalized the mercenaries could and
did become. It shows too how Hoare's leadership was necessarily harsh. Had
it not been, he would in all likelihood have lost control. And comparison of
his actions at Lubutu and Stanleyville show dramatically how ultimately his
decisions were based not on some impartial, abstract sense of absolute justice,
but on a harsh assessment of how best to maintain control over a group of
hired soldiers whose dominant motivation was financial gain and personal
survival.

However, the weeks which followed the capture of 'Stan' were taken up
with activities which did much to improve the light in which the mercenaries
were seen by the world at large. As they rescued priests, nuns, missionaries
and other European civilians held by the Simbas throughout the
neighbouring district, so they were portrayed in the press and on television
as heroic rescuers rather than the ruthless paid killers which had previously
been their public persona.

But the winds of change were, it seemed, blowing hard through 5
Commando. Some 150 new recruits were flown in to fill the large gaps which
had appeared throughout the ranks; death and injury had taken their toll,
but so too had desertion. Indeed, disillusionment reached to the very top, for

*An old woman whose house in Stanleyville had been destroyed in the fighting is a cause for mercenary concern (Camera Press).*

on Boxing Day Hoare himself began the process of handing over the reins of command to one of his Captains, Ian Gordon. Hoare, like many of his men, had had enough after six months in the Congo. It was the sort of warfare which sapped the spirit of the soldiers, and Hoare was also irked by the lack of military independence which he was forced to endure. His confidence in his employer was also shaken by the knowledge that despite the contracts which they had all signed, none of the dependants of those mercenaries killed had received the payments which were due to them. However, after a personal interview with Tshombe, after a meeting with his Chief-of-Staff General Mobutu (who promised him an independent command of a unified 5 Command), and after a fourteen-day holiday, Hoare returned to Stanleyville fully invigorated, and with the new rank of Lieutenant-Colonel he took charge of 5 Commando again.

It was not just Hoare who was invigorated. The fall of Stan, far from bringing the rebels to their knees, served to spark their foreign supporters into positive action. Egypt and Algeria were prominent among those who despatched considerably quantities of vehicles, arms and ammunition to

**Right** *Two sides of the mercenaries' campaign — the rescuing of a Belgian missionary...* (Camera Press).

**Below**...*and the ruthless killing of Simbas* (Rex Features).

**Left** *When mercenaries occupied Asangi Mission, they rescued a number of black nuns...*(Camera Press).

*...and smashed the Lumumba Memorial there* (Camera Press).

*General Mobuto, C-in-C of the Congolese Army* (Camera Press).

them, so that Hoare found himself faced by an enemy much better equipped than previously.

In accordance with General Mobutu's promises, Hoare was given overall command of the area designated Operations North-East. His task was to crush all rebel resistance there, and in particular to close the borders with Uganda and Sudan, thereby depriving the Simbas of help from outside the Congo. He was given charge of a two-battalion group which included 5 Commando, but before he could exercise his new authority in the field of battle he had first to concentrate on knocking his new recruits into shape. This was not as straightforward a task as he might have hoped for. Thus in the middle of one night, he was awakened by one of his officers with the news that his men had mutinied. Mounted on the back of an armoured car, he managed to bring his men back under control, and convinced them that the money which should have reached their families back home had been held up merely by the administrative process. Although the dissatisfaction of his men was not unreasonable, he nevertheless took the opportunity to separate off twenty men who seemed to have been the principal architects of the mutiny and despatch them back to where they had come from.

Even this mini-purge did not guarantee him freedom from further trouble. Shortly afterwards, a dozen mercenaries attempted to steal equipment and arms and desert to the enemy. When they were apprehended, they explained that they believed that the Simbas would hire them as mercenaries at much better rates. Hoare nor surprisingly kicked them out too, and observed that

Although Hoare's men all signed comprehensive contracts of employment, pay was usually *very slow in coming through. By February 1965, the arrears were such that resentment developed into virtual mutiny. These photographs show some of the 'volunteers' waiting around, bored and irritable, to hear if money had at last been paid into their accounts. Some actually refused to repel a rebel attack, while one said that he might sign a second contract, but only to ensure not losing all the money owed to him. 'If I leave this country, there's not a chance of getting my money.' In the end, the money came through, but only at the eleventh hour. Hoare had to handle more than one such explosive situation — and generally did so very effectively* (The Photo Source).

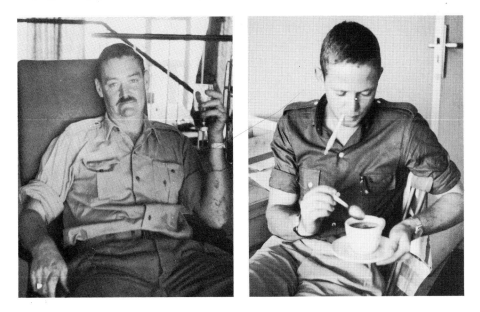

this was taking their calling as mercenaries 'a little too seriously'.

Once training had been completed, it took Hoare and his men just seven weeks of actual campaigning to carry out their task successfully. The climax of the operation was the capture of Watsa, a town famous for its gold mine, which had been an important source of finance for the rebel cause. Prominent amongst the mercenaries was the force which Hoare dubbed John-John, an élite body of 100 men led by Captain John Peters. A former member of the SAS, he was immensely tough in body and spirit, as well as being cool and deadly in action. He was in many respects the perfect soldier, though there were times when he overstepped the limits—as, for instance, when a Belgian mercenary attempted to sleep on his camp bed, and Peters stabbed him with a knife in the ensuing fight.

The force which Peters led was trained to his own very high standards, and was central to the success of this second period of campaigning, not least on the advance to Aba. After clearing out a substantial ambush on the approaches to Wawa, Hoare inspected his map and decided that the only place the enemy was likely to regroup before Aba was at the river Nzoro. If they once became established there, he was afraid that it might take several days to dislodge them, and that as a consequence the success of the whole campaign might be threatened. He therefore determined to advance as fast as possible to the river and seize the main bridge across it before the enemy had a chance to get dug in. During the drive, however, one of his men suddenly collapsed with blood pouring from a bullet wound in the head. Hoare immediately ordered a sweep of the nearby bush, but although it failed to turn up even a lone sniper, it did use up valuable time, with the consequence that when the sudden African darkness fell the column was still a few kilometres short of its target.

It was Hoare's strict rule after the Stanleyville nightmare march not to move through hostile territory by night, but he was extremely loathe to allow the enemy the whole of the night to regroup at the bridge. He therefore summoned Peters and explained the problem to him. He would never order him to do so, but if he was willing and could find some volunteers. . . Peters did not hesitate. He volunteered the whole of John-John and they moved straight out. Twenty minutes later they drove up to the Nzoro bridge just as a rebel column was starting to cross it. They opened fire, and immediately had the good fortune to hit an ammunition truck, which exploded in spectacular fashion. A fierce fire-fight ensued, at the end of which the entire rebel force was either dead or in flight. John-John's spoils included eleven vehicles loaded with equipment, weaponry and ammunition. This was a bonus, but the important thing as far as Hoare was concerned was that the bridge was now in his hands and the route to Aba was wide open. Indeed, this night-time action was the key to the whole campaign, and on the strength of it Peters was later promoted to the rank of Commandant by General Mobutu.

Peters' value was again demonstrated shortly after Hoare had declared the border with Sudan and Uganda closed. This declaration proved to be somewhat premature when the Simbas launched a cross-border attack on Aba, and Hoare, angered and embarrassed, decided that firmer measures were necessary. Again he called on Peters, this time entrusting him with a force of several hundred men and ordering him to sweep the country as far as Sudan clean of all Simbas, and if necessary to engage in hot pursuit of them across the frontier. It was risky from a diplomatic point of view, but as a military operation it proved to be highly successful. Peters pursued his enemy some eight miles into Sudan, destroyed their camp, and inflicted many casualties. As a result, the cross-border raids ceased.

Hoare's stock was never higher. Excellent relations existed between him and Mobutu, and between the mercenaries and the ANC troops. But there then occurred an incident which instantly soured the whole situation. Ironically, this involved Peters, the man whom Hoare most had to thank for his success.

Peters, who had been granted a week's compassionate leave, had to journey down to Paulis in order to catch a plane out of the country. For protection he took eight men with him as far as Paulis, although it was part of Hoare's standing orders that no mercenary should visit the town. Peters should have ordered his escort to return to Niangara without delay, but thinking that they had earned a bit of fun he authorized them to stay in Paulis overnight as long as they left the following morning. They went to a party, got into an argument, which developed into a fight, and in the ensuing confusion one of them shot and killed a Congolese adjutant. Although it was not clear where exactly the blame lay, it was immediately apparent that the incident would have wide repercussions.

The Katangese troops who had been under the command of the dead adjutant declared that they would not take part in the forthcoming campaign alongside white mercenaries, and a court of inquiry was convened. In the meantime, Peters' disobeying of orders, however well-meaning it may have been, could not be ignored. Mercenaries had to be seen to be liable to the same rules as anyone else, and Hoare had no option but to write to his most valued officer a painful letter telling him that his services would not be required until the whole matter had been cleared up.

Despite the dramatic deterioration in relations which this incident caused, Operation 'Violettes Imperiales' went ahead as planned. Indeed it was completed successfully and at some speed, with Bondo and Buta, the only sizeable towns still in rebel hands in the north-east, being captured without undue difficulty. The campaign was notable, however, for atrocities committed by both sides. The Simbas, anticipating defeat, killed their prisoners rather than let them be rescued, and the mercenaries took their revenge with a will. In his memoirs Hoare glosses over the details of much

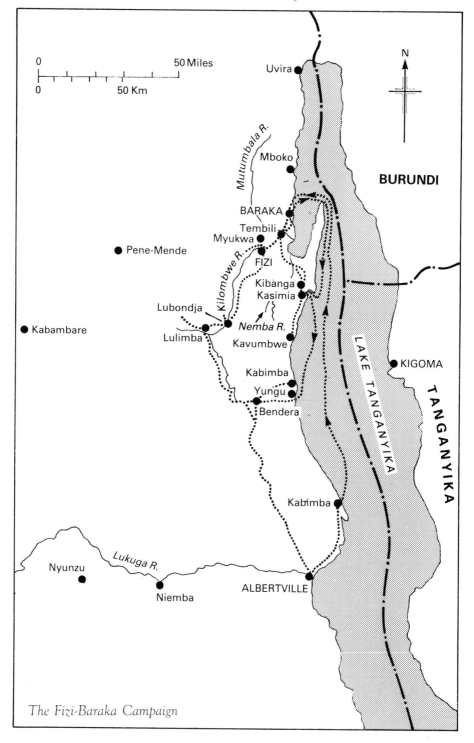

*The Fizi-Baraka Campaign*

of this, but he does relate how, when a group of prisoners attempted to escape, no attempt was made to recapture them. They were merely gunned down and left where they fell. When the mercenaries were drawing close to Buta, the 38 priests held captive there were shot and their bodies dumped in the river. The Simbas then disappeared into the bush, allowing Hoare and his men to capture the town without a shot being fired the following day. With that, the campaign was effectively over, but the taste of victory was bittersweet.

Hoare's second contract was approaching its termination date when he had another meeting with Tshombe. The Prime Minister congratulated him on all he had done, but told him that the situation in the south was causing him considerable concern. The rebels there were receiving much material assistance from Burundi across Lake Tanganyika, and were now strongly established in the Baraka-Fizi area. Hoare responded that he did not intend to renew his contract again. Tshombe applied some pressure: the job was only half done, and Hoare would again have overall command of the operation. Hoare succumbed, and agreed to serve a third spell, but only until Baraka-Fizi region had been cleared of rebels.

The campaign which confronted Hoare was the most daunting which he had so far faced, for a number of reasons: first, the Baraka-Fizi area was an extremely rugged mountain region, difficult of access and ideally suited to guerrilla tactics; second, his opponents were the Bahembi, perhaps the most warlike tribe in the Congo; furthermore, they were known to be assisted by a number of Cuban 'advisers'; and the local population was generally sympathetic to the rebel cause, something which had not been the case further north. Moreover, it was generally clear from recent rebel activity in the region that Hoare and his men could expect anything but an easy ride from opponents who were better equipped and led than any of the rebels whom Hoare had previously encountered.

Not surprisingly, there was no flood of eager new recruits. Hoare's recruiting officer in Johannesburg had told him that it was getting increasingly difficult to find suitable men to sign on, and although Hoare had himself received a number of letters from Britons eager to join 5 Commando, he never set up a recruiting office in Britain. He did, however, in a number of cases write back with the offer of a post if the recruit could make his own way to the Congo, and at his own expense. Despite the problems, the recruits did eventually come, and in some numbers, but the quality was extremely mixed. Indeed, Hoare pruned over 300 out and sent them packing. The new intake did at least include a few old hands from the first incarnation of 5 Commando, for which Hoare was grateful, though he did reject a Dane whom he recalled had a partiality for boiling the heads of his enemy!

Once the initial selection process was over, training commenced, initially at Albertville, but later also at Kabimba further to the north where

*A German mercenary, Pieter Stubbe, cleaning his gun on the banks of the Congo* (Camera Press).

occasional contact with enemy patrols could be expected. Apart from 5 Commando, Hoare also had under his control two battalions of the ANC, a small air force, and an even smaller navy. The former comprised twelve T-28s, piloted by Cubans again, four B-26s and a helicopter, while the latter consisted of a gunboat and six PT boats. Training progressed well, except for the almost predictable mutiny over pay, and Hoare received a late boost with the arrival of some old 5 Commando officers, including John Peters.

The strategic problem was how to dislodge the enemy. To strike north across country would mean making a frontal attack on the heavily defended Lulimba escarpment, and was almost bound to involve substantial losses. The alternative was an amphibious operation, and despite his earlier experiences of Lake Tanganyika it was this that Hoare opted for. He determined to turn the enemy defences by landing a force near Baraka; if he once captured that port, he would have cut off the rebels' supply route from across the lake. The key element in all this would be that of surprise—in particular he wanted to avoid the risks of an opposed landing—and he therefore kept his plan entirely to himself until three days beforehand, when he vouchsafed details to only his closest officers. The others were told nothing until they had embarked. To reinforce the deception, he even arranged for some 'Top Secret' papers to fall into enemy hands, which disclosed the details of a purported overland attack.

During the night of 25/26 September, Hoare embarked his men under the cover of darkness at Kabimba. The small navy which he had taken over had been increased by the addition of three other vessels, between them sufficient to transport a force of 200 men and eighteen armoured cars and jeeps. The infantry were divided into two groups—Force John-John under Peters (now with the rank of Commandant) and Force Oscar under Captain Hugh van Oppens. Furthermore, even as the small armada made its way up lake Tanganyika—out of sight of land to preserve the element of surprise—another force of a hundred men was marching overland under the command of Alastair Wicks. His task was primarily a diversionary one—to launch an attack on the Lulimba escarpment and pin down the enemy there while Hoare landed a few kilometres north of Baraka, captured the port, then moved on to first Fizi and finally Lulimba which, caught between two forces, would collapse under the pressure.

That, at least, was the theory. In practice, operations of any complexity rarely go strictly according to plan, and one which starts, as this did, with an amphibious, night-time landing was particularly liable to throw up problems. Nevertheless, the first problem was one which took Hoare very much by surprise. The weather. He had been assured that the lake was hardly ever rough, yet early on their second night afloat they ran into a terrific storm which very nearly scuppered the whole operation. (The irony of this, of course, though Hoare would hardly have appreciated it at the time, was that the mutinous Belgian whom Hoare had slugged with his pistol at Moba and later 'fixed forever' was proved to be right in his warnings about the dangers of the lake.)

Apart from making a number of the mercenaries very sick, the rough water greatly slowed down the boats. A group of seven mercenaries, trained and led by John Peters, had the task of recceing the beach in advance of the main force and signalling back if it was safe to land. They did not, however, set off for the beach until 03:00 hours, that is to say two hours behind schedule. This meant that if the main force was to land before it started to get light, there was absolutely no more time to waste. They at first proceeded in towards the shore in a PT boat, but later transferred to an assault boat, and with considerable difficulty managed to land on the shore (though not, as it happened, the intended beach). There they reconnoitred, found no enemy immediately at hand, and set up lights to show their position to Hoare. Hoare, however, was still, quite literally in the dark. The lights were invisible at such a distance in such conditions; the PT boat which had ferried the recce group some of the way had failed to return (its engine had failed); and he was also unable to make any radio contact with the beach.

If Hoare was metaphorically in the dark, he knew after an hour had passed that all too soon the physical darkness would begin to dissipate. He either had to abort the operation and abandon the recce party and mission PT boat, or he had to head for the shore and hope that they hit the right beach and that it was not defended. He decided to go ahead.

The five remaining PT boats took the first wave, commanded by van Oppens, forward towards the shore, and as they drew closer to the land they at last spotted the lights which the recce party had set up. By the time they reached the beach, however, the darkness was beginning to lift fast, and with it disappeared any chance of gaining the unopposed, surprise landing which Hoare had hoped for. Confirmation of this came as the PT boats disgorged their loads and turned to return to the larger vessels: suddenly the enemy opened up with a mixture of small arms, mortar and machine-gun fire. Speed was now of the essence, and the PT boats performed an invaluable service, ferrying successive waves of infantry to the beach until all 200 had landed by 05:15 hours. Then it was the turn of the jeeps and armoured cars, and once they were landed, all was ready for the advance to Baraka.

Now the weather, which had done its best to delay and put at risk the landing, and which had ensured that the element of surprise which Hoare had so sought would be lost, further interfered with Hoare's plans, for the cloud cover was so low that it made it impossible for Hoare's small air force

*Some well-equipped Simbas. When organized and led by Cubans, they proved a much tougher adversary for 5 Commando, notably at Baraka (The Photo Source).*

to render any assistance—assistance which the mercenaries needed against a fully alerted and extremely determined enemy.

They advanced at speed, the armoured cars in front, the jeeps, packed with soldiers, just behind. Their first aim was to secure the port area of Baraka so that further supplies of ammunition could be landed. While Force Oscar headed for the beach, Force John-John covered its flank and bore the brunt of the fighting in the process. But even Peters' much vaunted mercenaries were compelled to give ground before a much more numerous and very determined enemy. One of his Lieutenants was mortally wounded, and Peters himself was hit. For a while he stubbornly continued to give orders, but another of his Lieutenants, Sam Smallman, eventually had him evacuated to the rear while he took over command. In the meantime four PT boats had raced in carrying the ammunition which the mercenaries craved. Some of them had by now run out completely, a situation which reflects poorly on Hoare's planning and which indicates that he severely underestimated the degree of resistance which he would encounter at Baraka. Indeed, the sight of the PT boats unloading the ammunition spurred the rebels to even greater efforts, and a heavy machine-gun now began to rake the beach to such effect that the unloading of further stocks from the main supply boat was rendered impossible.

It was a critical position to be in, and the pendulum only swung the mercenaries' way when one of the other vessels, the *Ermans*, moved closer into shore and brought into play its 75 mm gun. The first shot was deadly and accurate, demolishing the building which housed the enemy machine-gun post. The pressure on the mercenaries eased, though only temporarily, but by the time the enemy had moved forward in yet another attack, enough ammunition had been unloaded to revive the mercenary cause. By the evening Hoare was able to feel that his position, if not comfortable, was at least firmly established. His casualties totalled four dead and seven wounded, compared with over a hundred enemy dead and an unknown number wounded. Hoare later described these as 'fearful losses'—a comment which would have had King Pyrrhus guffawing in his grave, but one which illustrates starkly how low is the level of casualties which a mercenary leader may find intolerable.

Over the next four days, it was the Cubans on both sides who played key roles. On the one hand, Cuban 'advisers' were instrumental in orchestrating the careful tacts of the revels; their presence was confirmed by the fact that Hoare's wireless operators picked up enemy radio messages in Spanish. On the other, with a sudden improvement in the weather and the lifting of the clouds, Hoare's Cuban pilots were able to fly low over the rebel positions and strafe them with considerable effect. This greatly eased the pressure on Hoare's small force, and after four days of this treatment the Cubans on the ground decided they had taken quite enough punishment from their own countrymen. This was immediately apparent the following day when the rebels resorted to the traditional tactics which Hoare had encountered elsewhere in the Congo. Instead of the careful probing attacks of previous days, they advanced in a large single mass, screaming the warcry 'Mai Mulele'. The mercenaries held their fire until the range was point-blank, then devastated their foes with a short spell of furious fire.

The tide had turned, and shortly afterwards Wicks, whom Hoare had radioed to abandon his attack on Lulimba, arrived with his hundred mercenaries and 300 ANC troops. With these reinforcements, and with the enemy abandoned by their Cuban 'advisers', Hoare now had the opportunity to break the back of rebel resistance in the area. The first target was Fizi, and with air support facilitating their advance, the mercenaries took it with remarkable ease—there were some ambushes that had to be cleared en route, but when they reached the town itself, they found it deserted. Lubondja also fell, as did the stronghold at Lulimba which, attacked from front and rear, proved a much less hard nut to crack than Hoare had feared. Kasimia, Kavumbwe, and the peninsula known as the Ubware followed in rapid succession—though the mercenaries suffered several casualties in the process—while further south two Belgian-led ANC battalions put the finishing touches to the campaign by capturing Yungu, the last bastion of rebel resistance.

Hoare's Congo adventure was now effectively over. Even as the mercenaries were overrunning this last major area of rebel resistance, Prime Minister Tshombe had been ousted from his position as Prime Minister by President Kasavubu. Tshombe had originally been appointed Prime Minister in the hope that he would save the Congo from the Simba rebellion, and now that he had achieved that, he was seen by Kasavubu as a threat to his own position as President. Nevertheless, Kasavubu did not long survive Tshombe's deposition since on 24 November General Mobutu, with the backing of the army, carried out a bloodless coup.

Although there was still work to be done in the Congo, Hoare, true to his promise, now finally relinquished command of 5 Commando for good, handing over the reins to John Peters. Mobutu, in a letter written just two days after the coup, wrote to Hoare in generous terms, thanking him for his service and expressing the wish that if the need arose in the future they might call on him again. 'La National Congolaise vous doit beaucoup.' ('The Congolese nation is greatly in your debt.') Hoare, accompanied by Wicks, paid a final visit to Tshombe and said his goodbyes. He then boarded a Boeing and flew home, his mercenary career apparently over. He could hardly then have guessed that some years later he would burst back into the headlines as the leader of an abortive coup against the President of the Seychelles, and would end up as a consequence in a South African prison.

*Joseph Kasavubu, President of the Congo from 1960 to 1965, who was deposed by Mobutu shortly before Hoare left the Congo for good (Camera Press).*

## Congo climax

Mercenary activity continued in the Congo for some time after the departure of Mike Hoare, until it climaxed spectacularly in a mercenary revolt in 1967. By that year, there were two main mercenary forces: 6 Commando under Bob Denard, and 10 Commando under Jack Schramme. The latter, a Belgian, was strongly positioned in the Marienna region where he had his own plantation, and wielded considerable local power. When President Mobutu asked Denard to disarm Schramme's troops, Denard refused, and after consulting with Schramme the two men decided to stage an uprising against their employer. After initial success, things began to go wrong for them, and by the second week of July Denard was injured and out of action, and Schramme isolated in Stanleyville. The latter and his men then disappeared into the bush, apparently resigned to defeat, but reappeared dramatically on 9 August at Bukavu the ANC defenders of which fled with virtually no attempt to resist. There Schramme stayed, with some 150 mercenaries and 800 Katangese, for three months. The ANC launched a ferocious attack at the end of October, but Schramme's men just managed to hold them off in two days of desperate fighting.

Meanwhile, on 1 November, Denard invaded Katanga from the South, in

**Above** *Two mercenaries drive through Bukavu shortly after its capture* (The Photo Source).

**Left** *Col 'Bob' Denard, in full uniform, speaks with General Mobuto at his villa in Kinshasa* (Camera Press).

**Below** *A mercenary and two Katangese outside Bukavu* (The Photo Source).

**Above** *ANC troops come and surrender their weapons to Schramme's men (The Photo Source).*

**Below** *ANC troops are searched and given refreshments. They have just crossed over the bridge from Rwanda (The Photo Source).*

**Above** *A white mercenary supervises the setting up of an anti-aircraft gun* (The Photo Source).

**Below** *Mercenaries in Bukavu* (The Photo Source).

**Above** *A mortar emplacement, part of the ring of defensive positions made by Schramme's men around Bukavu* (The Photo Source).

**Below left and above** *Schramme's disarmed mercenaries and Katangese wait under guard in Rwanda to learn if they will be sent back to face trial in the Congo. In the end, after five months, they flew to freedom, though Schramme himself was tried in Belgium; he was allowed out of the country on bail and disappeared. The Katangese were 'resettled' in the Congo, but were probably massacred by Mobutu* (The Photo Source).

the hope of raising rebellion there, and so drawing ANC forces away from Bukavu, but his campaign collapsed on 4 November, the same day as Schramme was forced to withdraw from Bukavu across the nearby border to Rwanda, where his men were promptly disarmed and interned. President Mobutu demanded that they be sent back to the Congo to be tried, but in April 1968 they were finally flown out of Rwanda and deposited in various cities around Europe.

## Chapter 2

# Angolan tragedy

'I only went to Angola because I couldn't get a job. I needed the money and a job in Angola sounded interesting.' Barry Freeman.

Freeman's hopes that service in Angola would prove interesting were fulfilled in a manner that exceeded his wildest nightmares. He was one of many Britons who found the prospect of earning £150 a week serving in the right-wing FNLA forces of Holden Roberto irresistible. Yet once out in Angola he quickly came to realize that he was not on to a winner. The left-wing, Cuban-backed MPLA were much better equipped and organized than

*You can bring enemies together, but you can't force them to be friends. Here, President Kenyatta hosts a meeting of UNITA leader Jonas Savimbi, MPLA leader Neto (right) and (left) Holden Roberto of the FNLA (Camera Press).*

the FNLA; their troops were more numerous and their morale was much higher. Furthermore, by the time the British mercenaries began to arrive in Kinshasa, Zaire, just across the northern border of Angola, the military situation of the FNLA was desperate. Indeed, it is easy to see in retrospect that a couple of hundred soldiers, hastily hired and in some cases hopelessly ill-equipped for the war into which they were pitched, were on a hiding to nothing. They were too few, too badly prepared, and too late.

The nightmarish element of Freeman's experience, however, had little to do with the MPLA and everything to do with his fellow mercenaries. For he found himself compelled, according to his own account, to take an active part in the 'execution' of fourteen of his comrades-in-arms. This horrific incident, once it became known, brought the full glare of the world's Press down upon the heads of the mercenaries, though the media had already given much coverage to the recruitment of mercenaries in Britain. Indeed they had provided the recruiters, Security Advisory Service, with much free publicity which had greatly assisted them in finding recruits. In some cases, newspapers had actually provided callers with the phone number of SAS.

In military terms, the mercenaries had a minimal effect on the course of events. They were unable to halt the advance of the MPLA forces to the Angola-Zaire border, and within a short time those who evaded death or capture were making their way back through customs at Heathrow. This was not the end of the story, however, for President Neto of Angola forced the

*Northern Angola*

whole issue of mercenary service back into the limelight by his decision to hold a trial of thirteen captured mercenaries. World attention was guaranteed by the surprise fact that one of the defendants was none other than Costas Georgiou, otherwise known as 'Callan', the man who had ordered the killing of the fourteen British mercenaries. His appearance was a surprise because he had been badly wounded in an ambush shortly after that incident and had gone missing. It had been presumed that he had either died of his wounds or had been finished off by the Angolans. He and his twelve fellow defendants were found guilty of the charge of 'mercenarism', and he was one of four condemned to death. Despite appeals for clemency, they were duly executed and the rest imprisoned.

The whole affair not only brought into question the morality of being a mercenary, but also threw much light on the rather mysterious and, as it was revealed, rather shabby world of the modern soldier of fortune. The notoriety of what happened in northern Angola in early 1976 should not, however, blind one to the fact that mercenaries continue to operate in Angola to the present day.

## Recruitment

Towards the end of 1975, a self-styled 'Dr' Donald Belford placed a newspaper advertisement offering 'a job overseas' for men with military experience. Belford was himself ex-Army, and had made several visits to Angola. There he had proved very useful to the FNLA, a liberation movement struggling to free that country from its Portuguese rulers. His value, however, was as a medic rather than as a soldier (hence the title of 'Dr' by which the Angolans addressed him, and which he assumed in England too), and he had established such a good relationship with the FNLA leader, Holden Roberto, that he had been appointed his representative in Britain.

The FNLA was not the only liberation movement in Angola, however. It had two rivals, UNITA led by Jonas Savimbi, and the Russian- and Cuban-backed MPLA. And when Independence Day came on 11 November 1975, it was the MPLA who, thanks above all to the several thousand Cubans in their forces, held the dominant position in the country. Indeed the FNLA, having suffered a severe defeat on the very eve of independence, were in a sore plight and were desperately short of money with which to prosecute their cause.

This was the situation when Belford's newspaper advertisement appeared. It prompted a reply from a certain Nicholas Hall, who offered Belford the services of himself and three friends. All four of them, he could truthfully assert, had formerly been in the crack 1st Parachute Regiment, and in that respect they were ideal for the work which Belford had in mind—namely assisting the FNLA in their fight against the MPLA. Indeed, one of them, Costas Georgiou, had been a star of the regiment. In another respect, however, they

*Holden Roberto, FNLA leader, flanked by aides and soldiers* (GAMMA/Spooner).

were far from ideal, for three of the quartet had been dishonourably discharged from the Paras. Georgiou (whom I shall refer to hereafter as 'Callan', the anglicized name by which he was soon to achieve worldwide notoriety) and Michael Wainhouse had been found guilty of the armed robbery of post offices during a tour of duty in Northern Ireland and sentenced to five years' imprisonment, while Hall himself had received a two-year sentence for selling arms to the outlawed Ulster Volunteer Force. The odd man out was one Charles Christodolou, though he was soon to prove himself no saint in Angola where he gained a reputation for callousness and cruelty second to none.

When Belford explained the situation to the quartet, they expressed great enthusiasm, both for the chance of escaping from a hum-drum life as builders and for the opportunity to help the FNLA—Hall in particular was vehemently anti-Communist. However, at this stage Belford was extremely short of funds, so that even when Holden Roberto informed him that he was happy to accept the services of the four ex-Paras, he was able to fly only one of them out. The one chosen was Callan—after he had demonstrated his devotion to the cause by setting fire to the room in London which served as the MPLA headquarters there—and at the beginning of December he flew out of Heathrow in the company of Belford and his bodyguard Colin Taylor.

Callan may have excelled in the trade of killing, but in the early days of his time in Angola it was to the saving of life that he dedicated himself. Based in the front-line town of Cremona, he proved of great value to Belford: he organized the cleaning up of the dirty hospital which was crowded out with casualties from the fighting; he assisted the 'doctor' in the numerous operations—many involving amputations—which were necessary; and he also made regular sorties in the ambulance, picking up and bringing back to the hospital many who would otherwise have died.

In mid-December, Belford and Taylor returned to England, but Callan stayed on in Cremona until, a few days after Christmas, he awoke one morning to find that he had overslept. His first thought was to find and upbraid the man deputed to wake him up—until, that is, he looked out of the window and saw, apparently only fifty yards away, a Russian T-34 tank. The FNLA, without warning him, had abandoned the town overnight, allowing the MPLA forces to roll in without a shot being fired. Even as he made his escape in Volkswagen car, Callan resolved to abandon the medical life and return to the business which he knew best—soldiering. He caught up with the FNLA at Negage, and there enlisted the help of two Portuguese mercenaries, an ex-boxer called Madeira, and Lopez. The town was threatened by a column of some 600 soldiers supported by four T-34s and four of the multiple rocket-launchers, mounted on lorries, known as Stalin's Organs. The odds against Callan were ridiculous, but in one respect they were to his advantage: the enemy had stopped advancing and was encamped a few miles south of Negage. (This was to allow a force of Portuguese fighting with the MPLA to infiltrate in a wide arc round to the rear of Negage where they were intending to ambuscade the road and cut off any possible retreat; but Callan was not aware of this.) Callan was, therefore, well placed to take the initiative, and this he did with remarkable effect. He and his two comrades stalked the enemy encampment without being detected. Then, while Madeira and Lopez opened up with machine-guns upon the astounded soldiery, Callan himself, apparently displaying an almost insane coolness, concentrated on the vehicles, firing anti-tank rockets into the T-34s and the Stalin's Organs. One of the latter exploded with such devastating force that when the threesome beat a hasty retreat they left behind some sixty dead and many more wounded. Although this remarkable surprise attack delayed rather than prevented the capture of Negage, it did have more far-reaching consequences in that it forced the US Central Intelligence Agency to reappraise the situation.

Ever since Cuban soldiers began to flood into Angola to support the Marxist MPLA, the American administration had been watching the situation there with increasing anxiety. The CIA had vast sums of money at its disposal, but had been unwilling to start hiring white mercenaries because of the possible political repercussions. Yet in the weeks which followed

**Above** *Cuban soldiers serving in Angola — they were essential to the MPLA cause* (GAMMA/Spooner).

**Below** *MPLA troops photographed in January 1976* (The Photo Source).

independence, the performance of the FNLA troops was abysmal, so much so that by the end of December it seemed to be only a matter of a few weeks before the war in the north would be concluded. What Callan's three-man attack did was to demonstrate to the CIA a clear alternative to letting events take their course: a few hundred mercenaries with the right military background might have a real chance of halting the MPLA's run of success and putting some much-needed backbone into Holden Roberto's men. One British Para of outstanding military ability was already available, three others were waiting in England for tickets to bring them to Angola, and who knows how many others might respond to the promise of action and money?

A few days after Callan's exploit, on 5 January, Wainhouse, Hall and Christodoulou flew into Kinshasa. Talks were held between the four friends, the CIA and Holden Roberto. The head of CIA operations in the area was a Frenchman known as Jean-Pierre, and nicknamed General Custer because of his long fair hair and moustache. It was he, according to the not always reliable account of Tomkins and Dempster, who urged Roberto to appoint Callan field-commander of his forces. Hall, we are told, sat in the corner temporarily forgotten (the others were not present) and 'was amazed at Jean-Pierre's recommendation. He thought it was a terrible mistake. But no-one asked his opinion and he kept his thoughts to himself.' (He obviously did not keep them to himself later! Hall perhaps gets unduly favourable coverage in Tomkins and Dempster's account.) Anyway, whatever Hall's real or supposed misgivings at the time, Callan was appointed Colonel and given the task of organizing the FNLA military effort from their base of San Salvador. Wainhouse and Christodoulou were each given the rank of Captain, while Hall, promoted to Major, was instructed to return to Britain with $25,000 provided by the CIA. His mission was to hire 25 mercenaries and return with them to Angola as soon as possible. Hall himself apparently turned down Roberto's offer of a cash payment at this stage, on the grounds that he and his friends were fighting for the cause. Nevertheless, when offered a piece of property in Angola after the war, he requested the coffee plantation of a personal enemy of Roberto which had been mentioned in a previous conversation—all 132,000 acres of it. Roberto agreed to this: 'It's yours if we win the war'.

Hall arrived in London on 11 January and was faced with the problem of how to find his mercenaries. He had exaggerated his own military contacts, and his initial attempts drew a blank. Yet there was one man in England who was in a position to help him. That man was John Banks, himself an ex-Para, though from the 2nd rather than the 1st Regiment. He had been featured in an article in the *Sunday Times* by Tony Geraghty six months previously, and it was Geraghty who apparently put Hall in touch with him—doubtless he scented the sort of scoop which every journalist craves.

Banks had served in the Paras from 1962 to 1969. Like Callan, he took to life in the roughest of regiments, and passed out at Aldershot as the best recruit of his intake. According to his own account he became progressively disillusioned with the shrinking role of the British Army in the world, and the decreasing prospects of action, though in his autobiography he glosses over the reason for his departure from the Army—dishonourable discharge after being convicted of driving without a licence or insurance. He tried the inevitable building trade, but his first job ended with him flooring his boss. He also tried lorry driving for a while, but it was active service which most appealed to him, whether smuggling persons over the East-West German border, going on deep penetration missions in Vietnam, or fighting with the Kurds in the Middle East. Then in the middle of 1975 he was approached by a man called Charles Grange who asked him if he could get together a force of mercenaries. When he put out a newspaper advertisement asking for ex-SAS, Paratroopers and Commandos 'for interesting work abroad', it attracted a barrage of phone calls, and when he held a meeting for all concerned in the Regents Centre Hotel, about 120 men attended. The terms of service which he revealed were good—£150 per week and life insurance of £25,000—but the job was unusual in that it involved making attacks on white Rhodesia. Banks commented that he didn't know how his recruits would react to fighting white soldiers 'for a black boss', but as he said 'money talks very loud to out of work ex-soldiers' and in the event only three backed out when the nature of the mission was revealed. In the end, however, it all came to nothing; an advance party of seventeen, holed up for a weekend at the Sky Line Hotel waiting for their flight out, went, as Banks put it, 'berserk' in an orgy of drinking and sex, with the result that their would-be employer called the whole operation off.

Nothing daunted, Banks decided to make use of the military expertise which he had tapped, and set up his version of the SAS—Security Advisory Services—a company which claimed to provide a complete anti-terrorist security service. (It also mendaciously claimed in its brochure to have been formed in 1970.) Banks states that a number of potential clients, including the American computer giant IBM, British American Tobacco, and various London hotels, were highly impressed by what SAS had to offer, but that 'the police warned them off. Someone in authority was putting the block on us every way that we turned because of our previous mercenary involvement.'

This, then, was the situation when Banks was approached by Hall round about 15 January 1976. Thus, when he was told that the immediate requirement was for a small group of ex-professional soldiers, and that advances of money were available both for recruits and recruiters, he knew exactly where to look. On 16 January, for instance, he found Derek Barker and some other ex-Para mates drinking in the Queens Hotel, Aldershot, and had no difficulty in persuading them to join the mission. He was able to offer them a minimum of £150 a week, more if they were deemed suitable to be officers (none of the

British mercenaries recruited for Angola had been a commissioned officer in the British Army, however), while Banks and his fellow recruiters received £200 per man recruited. The money which Banks advanced them consisted of pristine dollar bills, and he warned them to shuffle them about in order to break up the sequences. He also told them that it came from the CIA.

The military background of the nineteen men whom Banks rounded up at short notice was impressive—most were ex-Paras or ex-Special Air Services. They included Peter McAleese, formerly a Sergeant in the SAS and now appointed in command of the party; Sammy Copeland, Derek Barker and Barry Freeman, all of whose names will recur more than once in the following pages. Not that they were all angels in disguise. Barker had done stretches in gaol in 1969 and 1971, and was at this time on bail following an offence committed two months earlier, and was meant to report daily to his local police station. He was renowned for his liking for pub fights, in which he would break a beer bottle over his opponent's head and then use the broken end as an improvized weapon. Another recruit with a past was Dave Tomkins, who had a string of convictions behind him, mostly for safe blowing. He was one of only two men in this first batch who had not been in the army, but was considered useful as an explosives expert. Banks found him in a Camberley nightclub in the early hours of 17 January. He had just 56 pence in his pocket at the time. When Banks told him he had got a job lined up, Tomkins was sceptical—he had had experience of Bank's schemes in the past—but when Banks then proceeded to wave a wadge of notes in front of his nose, all scepticism fled. 'Whatever it is, count me in.'

Hall and the nineteen new recruits flew out of Heathrow on the evening of 18 January, while Banks stayed behind to continue hiring as many mercenaries as he could find. There was a brief hitch at the airport when McAleese handed over a form with the mercenaries' photographs to the passport control officer, only to be told that the form was rubbish. According to Barker, McAleese then 'said something to him that I didn't hear and the passport officer then picked up a phone, talked to someone for about a minute, and said it was OK, we could go through'. Through they went, and within a short while the Manchester Social Club, as they called themselves, was in the air and en route for Angola—from where a number would never return.

Banks now set to his task with a will. He was greatly assisted in this by the newspapers, indeed the very newspapers who would soon be reviling him for his part in the tragedy that was to come. First of all they helped him by the enormous and detailed publicity which they provided—he could not have paid for better advertising! Many of those who flew to Angola later admitted that their interest was initially kindled by the detailed newspaper reports which gave details of SAS and of the amounts of money to be earned. The case of John Nammock and Andy Holland is typical. Holland's attention was first attracted by the newspapers, and he asked his friend Nammock if he was interested in going to Angola with him. The nineteen-year-old Nammock had no military background, but said he would be interested if he could work in the hospitals. Holland thereupon rang the *Sun* newspaper, and was actually given SAS's phone number.

But if the media made Banks' job of recruiting much easier, it is also the case that Banks and his colleagues, pressured by a shortage of time and seduced by the prospects of a £200 commission per man, made little if any effort either to vet applicants for suitability, or to make it clear to them exactly what they could expect to encounter in Angola. At the time of the trial of the thirteen captured mercenaries, Banks was asked on television if he felt at all guilty about the Britons involved. He replied: 'Every man knew he was going to war. Every African war is very, very dirty. . . They took their chances of being killed, maimed, wounded or captured, the same as any other man.' But this is not convincing. First, the evidence suggests very strongly that the fact was that many of the recruits just did not know what they were letting themselves in for. Secondly, if Banks knew it was bound to be a dirty war, how could he justify sending people to fight in it who were not trained for it?

Take the case of David Smith, just seventeen years of age. He later said that he made no attempt to hide his age (and if he had, his lie would surely have been transparent), yet he was recruited for this 'dirty war'. So too, as we have seen, was Nammock, not quite as young but equally ill-equipped to cope with the situation into which he was pitched. Another recruit, Wainright, admitted to a fellow traveller on the plane out to Kinshasa that he had never been in the Army and just wanted to escape from the police. It is also the case that at the other end of the scale, the 'veterans' were by no means all ex-Paras in the prime of their lives; of those who were later massacred on Callan's orders, a couple had merely served short spells in the Royal Navy as submariners—hardly suitable preparation for an African land war—while another, 'Jock' McCartney, was a former Sergeant-Major in his fifties who, while he may have expected to be involved in training, was recruited by Banks above all for his fluency in Russian which he anticipated might be useful in the interrogation of prisoners and intercepting enemy radio messages.

Indeed it is clear that, despite Banks' disclaimer that everyone knew what they were letting themselves in for, this just was not the case. Nammock claimed at his trial that he had not even heard of Angola until he applied to SAS, and though the jury was amazed by such a remark there is no reason to disbelieve it. Indeed it would be surprising if men as young and naive as Smith and himself had heard of Angola—until it started to make the front pages of the tabloids. Furthermore, the indications are strong that Banks did not spell out in any great detail what they could expect to encounter. Jock

McCartney, while expecting to be doing military work, seems to have supposed that they would involve training local FNLA troops—instead he was required by Callan to go straight into front-line action; he refused, and so was shot with the others on Callan's orders. Some of the mercenaries were even told by Banks that it was for their non-military skills that he was recruiting them, and he led them to understand that they would not be required to fight. One such man was Terry White, a car salesman who flew in his spare time and expected to be employed as a non-combatant pilot; another was Roger Jenkinson, a mechanic who was told he would be involved in teaching the Angolans the technicalities of vehicle maintenance and repair. Certainly there was a need for such skills, but they were not the skills which Callan was expecting, nor indeed what Holden Roberto was thinking of when he originally asked Hall if he could recruit him a whole regiment of Paras. It is hard not to gain the impression that Banks was happy to let the recruits believe what they wanted to believe, as long as he got them to sign on the dotted line (and so picked up his commission). Not that everyone was convinced by Banks. Colin Evans told me that he was pretty sure that he would end up fighting, though Banks told him and the others that they would be involved in training. 'It doesn't take much common sense to know when a bloke's telling lies.' But for Evans, a desperate shortage of money and severe personal problems outweighed any worries he had about what Angola might hold in store.

Even Barker, the experienced ex-Para who went out with the first batch of recruits, asserted at his trial that 'we was told we was to go to Angola, West Africa, to help train an army of natives whose morale was very low. . . We thought this job we was going to do. . .was OK seeing I was out of work and things was expensive in England. . . I was wanted by the police for assault in December 1975 and I was on a £200 sterling bail.' Barker had good reason to make out at his trial that he was expecting to be involved in training rather than fighting, but by and large his statement has a ring of truth, and it seems to encapsulate the ignorance and motives of most of the recruits. He and the safe-blower Tomkins, as we have seen, were both glad to go anywhere to get away from the police in England, and they were certainly not unique; and the lure of cash obviously weighed very heavily with many of them, so much so that as a consequence they were only too ready to believe that the work they were going out to do was not particularly hazardous; like Freeman, quoted at the beginning of this chapter and also short of money, the majority of recruits seem to have found the prospect of work abroad in Angola 'interesting', even though their knowledge of Angola, and of the work which would be required of them, was minimal.

### Massacre
After a week of frantic activity on the part of Banks and his fellow recruiters,

on Wednesday 28 January two groups of mercenaries, totalling nearly a hundred men, flew out of Heathrow bound for Kinshasa, Zaire. Banks himself led one group, while an unnamed spokesman for Security Advisory Services predicted that 'this is just a spearhead, and there could be a lot more following'. His confidence did not seem to be misplaced, especially when, the next day and as a result of the blaze of publicity given to the venture, some 300 phone calls were received by the SAS telephonist from people interested in jumping on to the bandwagon.

The leader-writer of the *Times* newspaper, with some pomposity, declared that the government was right to keep out of the affair. 'British interests are not involved to any great extent. If Englishmen want to join for the cause or the money they are free to do so. Labour MPs, some of the most respected of whom have the words International Brigade engraved on their hearts, should have no difficulty in appreciating that.' It is easy to see from the comfort of hindsight how peculiarly inappropriate such words were. High idealism was present in the breasts of few, if any, of the mercenaries; at the very time that the *Times* leader was being drafted in the comfort of London, extremely unpleasant things were going on in Angola, and within a very short span even more unpleasant happenings would occur (or rather, more

*Some of the nearly 100 mercenaries who embarked on two planes at Heathrow on 28 January. 'This is just a spearhead', one of Bank's associates commented (The Photo Source).*

newsworthy, for the casual massacre of unwilling mercenaries is hardly more
unpleasant than the out-of-hand killing of Angolans in which Callan had
been indulging since his promotion by Holden Roberto).

The first batch of mercenaries had not found the situation in Africa to be
entirely as they had been led to believe. The first thing to strike Tomkins,
almost literally, was the intensity of the heat; when he walked down the
aircraft steps in Kinshasa he felt as if he had walked into a solid wall of it—
and that was in the early evening, not the middle of the day. The second
thing was his defencelessness; none of the mercenaries were to feel happy
until they had weapons in their hands, yet when Holden Roberto and Hall
took them to the armoury a little later they were disappointed to discover
that the up-to-date equipment which they had been promised was in short
supply. There were only five Belgian-made FN 7.62 mm automatic rifles;
otherwise they had to rely on US rifles used in the Second World War.
Needless to say, all the rifles were filthy, and no cleaning materials were to
be found.

Soon the mercenaries were heading south, across the Zaire-Angola border
and to the town of Sao Salvador, the headquarters of the FNLA. Here they
first met up with Callan, with whom Dempster and Tomkins at least were
not impressed. They record how Callan, when he first looked over the new
arrivals, did so 'with unconcealed contempt'. Callan's feelings for the new
mercenaries were nothing compared to his attitude towards the black FNLA
troops under his control whom he viewed as untrustworthy and
incompetent, and treated with utter disdain and considerable violence. Now
that he had the backing of the new arrivals to add to the Portuguese soldiers
under his command, he took the opportunity to parade the black FNLA,
then order them to lay down their arms and strip. When he called for
volunteers, only fifty or so came forward; the rest he had driven to Quiende,
a few miles away. This gave the British a chance to replace their equipment
with that discarded by the Angolans. This time they had a much wider
choice, including Kalashnikov AK-47s and FN automatics, but again they
found the weaponry filthy. Even more indicative of the general incompetence
of the Angola soldiery, however, was the fact that many of the discarded
rifles were discovered to have the wrong ammunition jammed in their barrels.
It is not hard to understand why Callan preferred, in such circumstances, to
establish at least who was keen to fight for the FNLA cause. Dempster's own
most valuable find amongst all the discarded equipment, however, was not
an up-to-date rifle but an unbreakable metal water bottle; the plastic one with
which he had been issued earlier had broken when he jumped out of a lorry,
and subsequently it had taken only two hours of guard duty for him to
dehydrate so severely that he came close to the point of collapse.

The mercenaries' first taste of action was when word came in that the
Angolans at Quiende had mutinied. They rushed there, but encountered no

real resistance; some twenty blacks were apparently shot out of hand by Callan, the rest rounded up and disarmed again, and the whole of the armoury removed to Sao Salvador. Callan's management of the mutiny, ruthlessly efficient though it was, did not cause the recent arrivals to feel any great confidence in his leadership. Tomkins and Dempster record that at an earlier inspection Callan had 'taken every opportunity to abuse and humiliate his men', and distrust of his unpredictable behaviour was considerable. The casual way in which he, Christodoulou and Wainhouse were prepared to kill Angolans, often for no good reason, was unnerving at first, though Sammy Copeland at least was soon imitating them, and before long most of them seem to have become hardened to such callous brutality.

Christodoulou took great pleasure in recounting their various exploits: on one occasion, Callan, anxious to try out a Smith and Wesson .44 Magnum, did so by calling in a passing Angolan soldier and shooting him at point-blank range in the face; on another occasion an Angolan who cheerfully waved at Callan as he passed him in a jeep and addressed him as 'Camarade' was arrested and a little later shot as being unreliable; and near Maquela there was a bridge that had quickly become a favourite place from which to dispose of unwanted persons. Even if there is some exaggeration in the accounts of Callan's and the others' behaviour, there is no doubt that they are essentially true—and that their treatment of the Angolans, whether friendly or unfriendly to their cause, was erratically brutal.

Furthermore, it is indicative of the poor state of relations that developed initially between Callan and most of the new arrivals that when he ordered McAleese to take six mercenaries to the coastal town of Antonio do Zaire, Dempster and some of the others saw it not as a strategic move but as a ploy to remove from the main area of operations a man who was a potential threat to Callan's leadership. Indeed, on the evening of that same day, Thursday 23 January, Dempster and Tomkins sat down and discussed the practicalities of fleeing from Sao Salvador in a jeep—and the only thing which persuaded them not to make such a move was the thought of Callan, Wainhouse and Christodoulou coming after them in hot pursuit.

However, that same evening a telegram arrived from Holden Roberto. It informed Callan that the town of Damba had been captured by enemy forces and urged him to send reinforcements to Maquela do Zombo in order to prevent the MPLA/Cuban forces from breaking right through the FNLA front to the Zaire border. From that moment Dempster found himself far too busy to even think about escape, for one of the main requisites was as many serviceable vehicles as possible—and that was his area of responsibility. He spent most of the next thirty hours working flat out, preparing first two vehicles for McAleese's party, which left for Antonio do Zaire at dawn on the 24th, and then as many as he could for the main party, which drove out of Sao Salvador at 15:30 hours on the 25th.

The road to Maquela was hardly worthy of the name at the best of times, but now heavy rain made it highly treacherous. The progress of the convoy was therefore slow, and the lorry carrying the explosives which Tomkins had collected together turned over, much of the load being irrecoverable. Callan, typically, was the first to arrive at Maquela, and immediately set about putting into action his plans to counter the impending enemy attack.

The obvious way of approach for the MPLA forces was along the main Damba to Maquela road. However, branching off that road was another track which looped in a curve round Maquela, passed over the large Rio Zandi bridge, and then entered the town from the north. After first getting a report of enemy activity from the FNLA troops in Maquela, Callan drove out to the Rio Zandi bridge and ordered 'explosives' Tomkins to blow it up in order to prevent any possibility of the enemy using it to outflank his position. Tomkins, who was expecting a much smaller structure, had good reason to rue the fact that many of his explosives were buried in mud somewhere between Maquela and Sao Salvadore; he had great difficulty in detonating his first explosion which in any case only blew a hole in the road without rendering it impassable. However, a second detonation, early on Sunday 26th, brought down a complete span of the bridge.

Once Callan was satisfied that his rear was secure, he proceeded to take the initiative. After advancing along the main road to within about fifteen kilometres of Damba, he ordered the five-man 'killer' group which he had chosen to hide themselves amidst some thick scrub along the side of the road and wait for developments. They did not have too long to wait. An artillery barrage which fell short of their position was a prelude to the enemy advance. After about an hour silence suddenly descended, and soon after that Cuban infantry appeared on foot over the brow of the hill. They were followed by several jeeps crammed with more infantry, and they in turn were followed by three T-34 tanks. At the sight of the latter, the mercenaries felt decidedly uneasy, for Callan had left them without any transport to facilitate a speedy retreat. Perhaps Callan, anticipating their qualms, had done so deliberately, to ensure that they would not pull out without springing their ambush.

As things transpired, the mercenaries' fears were unjustified. As soon as they opened fire, the enemy turned in flight. While his four comrades concentrated on the infantry with their automatics, Dempster aimed for a tank with his rocket launcher. His first attempt failed by a distance, but it was enough to convince the tank commander that discretion was the better part of valour. As he turned his T-34, he presented Dempster with a tempting target, but again the rocket flew wide of its mark. Disgusted with his lack of success, Dempster grabbed his FN and fired after the fast disappearing infantry until they were out of sight. Silence fell, and it was some time before it dawned on the quintet that their fusillade had been so successful that far from counter-attacking, the enemy was withdrawing towards Damba in

Adherents of the MPLA attend an Instruction Centre whose curriculum includes political theory and military instruction. Despite this, Callan's mercenaries were not impressed by the quality of the opposition (The Photo Source).

search of reinforcements. A check of the battlefield revealed 21 dead, while the mercenaries were unscathed.

When Callan returned to learn of the success of the ambush, he determined to follow it up, and, after gathering together some more mercenaries and some FNLA troops, he pushed further forward towards Damba and set up another ambush. This time, however, the enemy did not oblige him by advancing into it, and eventually Callan called his men off. Indeed the first ambush had had a disproportionate effect on the MPLA forces, and it was to be some time before they attempted to engage Callan's men again. And in the meantime, in England, reinforcements were gathering.

These arrived at Kinshasa, under the personal leadership of Banks, on 29 January, and within hours they were all equipped with FN automatic rifles. The searing heat, which had so impressed Dempster when he first set foot on African soil, had an even more devastating effect on one of the older recruits, who collapsed with a heart attack. Meanwhile Banks had discussions with Holden Roberto concerning the recruiting of more mercenaries and then, to his credit, announced to the President that he would not allow his men to enter Angola until he had gone and had a look for himself. So it was that Banks, escorted by ten mercenaries, accompanied Roberto to Sao Salvador and there encountered Callan.

It was a tense meeting, for Banks had been warned by Hall that Callan had a grudge against him, and Callan was extremely suspicious of the man who he feared would attempt to ingratiate himself with Roberto in order to replace Callan as commander-in-chief in Angola. According to the account of Tomkins and Dempster, the exchange was opened by Banks.

'Is your name Callan?'

'Commandant Callan,' was the terse reply.

'My name is John Banks. . . I hear you've got a grudge against me?' The challenge in Banks' voice was unmistakable, but Callan was unimpressed and side-stepped the question.

'I've never heard of you in my life,' he lied.

The tension momentarily lessened, and the two men shook hands. Then Callan asked where the rest of the new recruits were.

'They don't come to the front until I know everything out here is okay. We haven't had any intelligence report.'

The words were a verbal slap in the face for Callan, and according to witnesses they almost drove him over the edge. For a few seconds, he was but a hair's breadth away from emptying his automatic rifle into Banks' body. Then, with a film director's timing, Copeland made his appearance from inside Holden Roberto's palace behind, his machine-gun at the ready. In response, several of the mercenaries who had accompanied Banks from Kinshasa aimed their weapons menacingly at Callan, but he, uncowed, began to berate them for threatening him. Banks asserted that they were his men, under his orders, and were as yet nothing to do with the commander of the FNLA forces. Argument flowed back and forth, and as it did the situation slowly defused.

This little drama had little to do with subsequent events, however. Within an hour, both participants had left town, their pride intact. Callan left on reconnaissance, while Banks returned to Kinshasa, though not before Copeland had threatened to kill him if the supplies which he had promised were not forthcoming. Banks was, apparently, satisfied with what he had seen in Sao Salvador, and later that same day his 96-man detachment left the capital of Zaire for Sao Salvador and then Maquela. They were not, however, accompanied by Banks, who flew back to London to undertake more recruitment. His departure came as a surprise, and appeared to many to be something akin to desertion. They had been expecting him to lead them in the field, and one individual commented bitterly that 'rats know when to abandon a sinking ship'.

It took almost two days of hard slog for the new recruits to reach Maquela, and almost immediately, early on Saturday 31 January, they were called out on parade by Callan. He then proceeded to make clear to them what his expectations were. Those with experience of the Paras or the Special Air Services were to join the three 'killer groups' under the command of himself, Christodoulou, and Copeland. Rules would be as in the British Army, and anyone breaking them could expect to be shot. He went on to outline the military situation, and to explain his proposed strategy which would involve penetrating the enemy lines and attempting to knock out the enemy tanks.

The mention of tanks was, apparently, the last straw for many of the newcomers. At first muted, then more openly, they began to voice their complaints. The elderly ex-Sergeant-Major recruited by Banks for his fluency in Russian, Andrew 'Jock' McCartney, stepped forward politely and said to Callan: 'Excuse me, Sir. I have made a mistake. I didn't realize what I was in for and I'm not cut out for this sort of thing.' Others protested that they hadn't been recruited to fight, and yet others that they had been promised that there would be a period to acclimatize and undergo training. It is not difficult to understand their reactions. A number of them had no military experience at all, and those who had were by no means all ex-Paras or ex-SAS. As we have already seen, many of those recruited by Banks had been motivated above all by the prospect of quick money; they knew little about Angola or what they might be letting themselves in for; nor had Banks been concerned to enlighten them. Indeed it seems clear that he had specifically told some that he was recruiting them for their non-military skills, not as soldiers. Thus young Nammock expected to be given medical duties (there was plenty of demand for those), Jenkinson mechanical ones, and White expected to be flying.

Callan's reaction to the complaints of the newcomers was one of extreme rage—nor is that surprising, especially considering his capacity for anger. He had been expecting a large draft of men with military experience, men who were willing and ready to fight. He desperately needed reinforcements for even the first, small draft had thinned out substantially. Two of them had recently gone missing and were presumed dead (one, McCandless, was dead, but the other, Lewis, was at that moment making his way wounded back to Maquela). Three others—Tomkins, Wainhouse, and Hussey—had had to be evacuated to Kinshasa. And seven others were still in the coastal town of Antonio do Zaire. Yet Callan was convinced, especially after the success which the five-man ambush had enjoyed, that the enemy could be beaten if only he had enough men to form 'killer groups' which would operate somewhat in the manner of guerrillas, springing ambushes and launching surprise attacks on hostile units. However, now that the much-needed reinforcements had arrived, they proved a severe disappointment to him as they complained about conditions and how they had not been hired to fight tanks.

Heated argument and discussion ensued, and culminated in Callan separating off 23 non-combatants from the others; these comprised not merely those who did not want to fight, but also some whom Callan decided were totally unsuited for action. The former included one ex-Para, Kevin Whirity, whose refusal to fight so appalled Callan that he threatened him with the words: 'If anyone dies, you'll be the first. Okay?' The latter included the two submariners whose presence in a force fighting a land war in Africa made even Callan laugh.

Callan ordered them all to strip, and invited the others to help themselves to whatever they wanted. 'Anything you need, take it off them over there. Kit, cigarettes, watches, rings, anything you want—take it.' Meanwhile, Dempster and Freeman kept their distance and casually speculated on what might be going to happen next, for they were by now well aware that stripping was often a prelude to an execution. But Callan, having humiliated the non-combatants, was at this stage more concerned with getting the other seventy-odd men into action than in taking reprisals. He told Dempster to take charge of the 23 and keep them busy in Maquela—'Give them plenty of shit!'—while he took the rest off to the base camp.

About noon the same day, Dempster came into possession of two important pieces of information. Firstly the Cessna which acted as the FNLA reconnaissance plane landed outside Maquela, and then, while Dempster drove out to question the pilot, a message from Holden Roberto came through on the radio. The pilot reported that he had spotted an armoured column on the Damba road; this was the one which Callan's men had ambushed earlier in the week, but now it was substantially reinforced and was about five kilometres south of the place known locally as Banana Junction. The radio message contained worse news: the town of Tomboco had fallen to a force of tanks and infantry. This was serious, as Callan realized when Dempster reported it to him, for it opened up the possibility of an attack on Sao Salvador from the south-west as well as the alternative of the enemy striking north to isolate McAleese's force in Antonio do Zaire.

Callan, nothing if not decisive, immediately set off for Tomboco with his own 'killer group' of some twenty men, leaving Copeland in charge of the remainder. Copeland, not to be outdone, decided to deal with the other threat himself. After outlining his plans to his men and giving them some weapons practice, he set off for the village of Quibocolo. Two of the last people to leave were Dempster and Freeman, and while they waited for their jeep to be repaired they visited the 23 non-combatants. They found them to be, not surprisingly, on edge and fearful that Callan might be going to shoot them when he returned. Dempster, by his own account, did his best to reassure them, and asked them why they did not want to fight. Those with suitable military backgrounds said they were disillusioned with the conditions and equipment, others complained they had been signed up to do non-military jobs.

This does not seem to have cut much ice with Dempster who, by his own account, urged them to get back into Callan's favour by volunteering to join the proposed attack that night. He said that he would be back in a couple of hours and that he would pick up then anyone who had changed his mind. This does not, however, entirely tally with the account given by his companion Freeman who related his story to a London journalist less than two weeks after the incident. According to him, 'if they saw trucks coming over the ridge above Maquela that night, it was possibly us coming back for rations'. A rather different version was given by Kevin Whirity, however, and this is of particular interest because he was one of the 23 non-combatants. He claimed that Dempster had said that he 'would try and get back around nightfall, but if anything came down the road after nightfall we would know it was the Cubans'. According to Whirity, Dempster asked if any of them wanted to join in an attack on the enemy, but when nobody volunteered he departed with a final warning: 'If by dark I don't come up that road, there'll be nothing coming but Cuban tanks, troops—they've even got their own bloody aircraft'.

A couple of hours passed, but Dempster and Freeman did not return. Meanwhile the non-combatants became increasingly twitchy. Whirity said that they noticed Brian Butcher and Ken Aitken, who had been left in charge of them, looking worried. 'They knew something was going on. You couldn't not know. Portuguese and black troops were coming in and at every key point they stationed a Portuguese or a black. There were some chaps on the far side of the compound, watching. Watching us. We were under guard.' Darkness fell. The non-combatants ate some food. Then they were ordered into the slit trenches. All of them were now armed for fear of an enemy attack. All of them were extremely edgy.

It was not until 22:00 hours that Freeman and Dempster set off back to Maquela, together with Tony Boddy and a man known as Max. As they approached, they could see no sign of lights and took this to mean that the non-combatants had settled down to sleep. Supposing that they would have left guards on watch, Freeman stood up in the Land Rover and flashed his torch as a sign that they were friendly. The wakeful non-combatants, however, when they saw the light and realized that a vehicle was approaching, jumped to the conclusion that it was hostile. Indeed, with their fears magnified by the dark and their imaginations beginning to run riot, they convinced themselves that the light which they could see was in fact the first in a column of enemy tanks. Whirity later recalled: 'To me, there was only one thing it could be. Tanks travelling at night use only one light. Somebody wondered if they were Dempster's patrol, but somebody who'd seen a bit of service said wheeled vehicles don't use only one light. "Them's tanks," he said. A wind started up and over it everyone imagined they could hear the clatter of tank tracks.'

So as the Land Rover drew near, 'all of a sudden all hell let loose'—or so it seemed to Freeman. A 66 mm anti-tank shell, fired by 22-year-old Phil Davies, smashed into the front of the vehicle, and was followed by a hail of small arms fire. The four occupants of the Land Rover, miraculously escaping injury, dived for cover. After about fifteen seconds the firing subsided and silence descended. The quartet, guessing that they had been mistaken for Cuban/MPLA forces, took the opportunity to shout out that they were British and to tell them not to fire, but their voices were immediately drowned by another fusillade of automatic fire. This convinced them that they had guessed wrong, and that the town must have fallen to the enemy. Tony Boddy and Max ran off the way they had come to report the situation to Copeland, while Dempster and Freeman decided to skirt round Maquela until they reached the Sao Salvador road and try and pick up information from the locals.

Meanwhile, the non-combatants, having loosed off their weapons against an invisible foe, had no intention of waiting to see what happened next. Instead they piled into three lorries and fled along the Sao Salvador road, off which after a few miles they branched north towards the safety of the Zaire border. Unfortunately for them, however, they ran straight into a detachment of FNLA troops under the command of an ex-SAS soldier— Terry Wilson. When he stopped them, they immediately poured out their story—which had already gained some remarkable embellishments: Maquela, they asserted, had fallen to the Cubans; it had been attacked by a large force; they had managed to knock out a couple of tanks before they had managed to retreat, but now all was lost; Copeland and his men must have been wiped out, and the only option was to flee to the security of Zaire. But Wilson was not the sort of soldier to give up as soon as the going got rough. Although he believed what he was told about the fall of Maquela, his first thought was to inform Callan of what had happened.

When the radio call came through, Callan was already on the way back from Tomboco. The report of its capture had proved wrong and he was therefore hurrying to rejoin Copeland. The news of the capture of Maquela, and of the destruction of Copeland's force, enforced an immediate change of plan. He told Wilson to set about blowing up a bridge on the Cuimbata road, to prevent the enemy outflanking them and cutting off their route of retreat to Zaire. The non-combatants were to come and meet him on the Sao Salvador road. The fact that they had apparently shown some fight before abandoning Maquela pleased Callan, and he hoped that they might be of some use in salvaging the situation.

But, while the non-combatants resignedly turned round and headed off to meet Callan, Copeland, Dempster and Freeman were hot in pursuit. It had been some time before Dempster and Freeman had discovered from the locals that Maquela was not in the hands of the MPLA, and when they reached the centre of the town they found Copeland already there. It was immediately clear that it must have been the non-combatants who had fired upon them, and this was confirmed by an Angolan mechanic called Joseph. According to Dempster he had noticed them loading up three lorries earlier in the evening; they had all been in combat gear and armed. Joseph had apparently fallen asleep, only to be woken by the sound of gunfire. He had then seen the non-combatants drive off in the three lorries. A check of the store room confirmed that the non-combatants had indeed loaded their lorries with all the essentials, and in particular that they had taken with them all the reserves of fuel.

'The bastards. . .they've legged it for Zaire, that's what they've done!', was Copeland's angry reaction. 'They knew you were coming back last night,' he said to Dempster. 'That's why they tried to top you, so you wouldn't give the alarm.' It was an understandable, though perhaps wrong, conclusion. The fact that they had loaded up the lorries so carefully implies at least that they were preparing for any eventuality, including flight to Zaire, but it seems less likely that they deliberately set out to kill Dempster, Freeman and the others. Rather, when they saw the single light of a vehicle approaching, they assumed it was an enemy tank, opened fire on it with everything they had, then bolted.

Whatever the precise truth, Copeland and the others were now hell bent on catching up with them, and within minutes they were tearing along the road out of Maquela in a Land Rover. Boddy was at the wheel, and Copeland at his side, while Dempster, Freeman and three others hung on for dear life in the back as Boddy, urged on by Copeland, drove like a man possessed. They soon came across one of the three lorries—it had been abandoned, on its side—but after a brief pause pressed on until they reached the fork in the road. Concluding that the fugitives were most likely to have turned north along the Cuimbata road towards the Zaire border, they took that route themselves. As they hurried on, however, their hopes began to dwindle— until they suddenly spotted a truck up ahead. This turned out, to their disappointment, to belong to Wilson and his detachment of FNLA soldiers. Wilson, for his part, was surprised to see Copeland and the others. He said he thought they had been killed, and he proceeded to tell them what the non-combatants had told him—about the 'Cuban' attack and how they bravely managed to destroy two tanks before being compelled to flee.

His listeners grew understandably enraged as he unfolded his version of events; for not only had the non-combatants nearly killed some of them but, to add insult to injury, they had turned their action into a tale of heroic resistance. However, when Wilson added that the non-combatants had now gone to rendezvous with Callan, Copeland gave a whoop of joy, and without further ado he, Dempster and the others drove off back the way they had come. After reaching the Sao Salvador road, they turned right and before long ran into Callan. He, like Wilson, had given them up for dead and could scarcely believe his eyes when Copeland jumped down from the Land Rover to greet him. It was a highly emotional meeting: Callan, his eyes moist with tears, hugged Copeland warmly, and could hardly speak for joy. But, as Copeland and the others told him what had really happened at Maquela, and as he realized the extent of the non-combatant's deceit, he grew furious, and swore in both Greek and English. 'Those bastards, trying to kill my men. . . I'll fuck 'em for good.' However, the non-combatants were now armed, and if Callan was going to disarm them physically, he would first have to do so metaphorically. So when he returned to where he had left them to dig in, he pretended to treat the whole business as almost ridiculous, and joked that they were now going to retake Maquela from the Cubans. So they all drove back to Maquela, and there he called out all his men on parade. These included the non-combatants, the rest of the British mercenaries drawn up separately, and Callan's Portuguese mercenaries who were so positioned, if Dempster is to be believed, as to cover all the British mercenaries and so thereby ensure that Callan's orders were carried out.

In fact, of the 25 non-combatants who had fled from Maquela, only twenty were present. One, Michael Mott, had gone on patrol as Christodoulou's driver, and four others, including Aitken and Butcher who had been in charge, had managed to slip away without being noticed. Callan ordered the twenty standing in front of him to lay down their arms and strip to their underpants. Meanwhile he berated them with a fierce denunciation of their behaviour, reminding them that the British Army punishment for mutiny and desertion was death. He asked who had fired the rocket at the Land Rover the previous evening. A young ex-soldier, Philip Davies, stepped forward.

'Me, Sir.'

The precise details of what happened next vary from account to account. According to Dempster, Callan, who had already drawn his Browning pistol, shot Davies at point-blank range in the forehead, and then twice more in the head as he fell. Freeman, speaking less than two weeks after the event, mentioned only two shots, the first in the neck, the second in the head, though Evans, speaking over ten years later, recalls Callan shooting three times in the head. According to Kevin Whirity, however, who was bent down undoing his boots right next to Davies, Callan first shot him in the leg. 'I felt blood and bits of leg splatter into my face. The boy fell against me and said: "Help me, Kevin," but I pushed him away. He fell back against the wall, and Callan shot him in the body and then in the head, and finished him off.' Everyone, according to Evans, was dumbfounded by the remarkable and horrific turn of events. 'We just could not believe that he had shot one of his own men.'

Callan now offered a final chance to the non-combatants to fight. (Dempster says that it was he who suggested this to Callan.) He turned to Whirity and said: 'You, Para, are you prepared to soldier?'

'Yes, Sir,' came the reply.

Whirity then pointed to his friend Dave Payden.

'What about him? He's a good soldier.'

Callan called him out, and then four others. One, Kevin Marchant, was to be Callan's driver, but the others were told that they would be manning the lead vehicle in the next attack—and would thereby be at considerable risk, especially if they ran into an ambush.

Turning back to the remaining thirteen non-combatants, now in varying stages of undress, Callan ordered them to finish stripping. When Jock McCartney started to complain, Copeland fired a burst from his automatic near his feet. Then Callan pronounced sentence: 'You stupid cunts—all you had to do was behave yourselves and you'd all have gone home safe. . . Instead you're all going to die.'

Then he addressed Copeland: 'Take them out of town. You know what to do.' Copeland by all accounts, laughed. Certainly as the wretched non-combatants were herded aboard the Dodge lorry which was to take them to their execution, Callan's Sergeant-Major indulged in some vicious taunting. He told them that they should have volunteered because in five minutes they would all be dead. Brandishing a grenade-launcher at McCartney he told him: 'I'm going to try this one out on you'.

The Dodge was driven by a Portuguese mercenary called Uzio. At his side sat Dempster, and in a Land Rover behind came Copeland, the other two mercenaries who had nearly been killed by the non-combatants—namely Freeman and Boddy (Max was absent)—and Paul Aves and Andy McKenzie who had also been deputized by Callan to join the execution squad. About three miles out, they stopped. Copeland lined up the non-combatants facing away from the vehicles down the valley. Standing behind them were the execution party. It is difficult to be sure what the various members were feeling. Both Freeman and Dempster stress in their accounts that their participation was unwilling, though it is hard to believe that they felt too much sympathy for men who had nearly killed them and then attempted to abandon them with no supplies. Indeed Dempster admits as much, but added that he had no wish to take part in a cold-blooded murder. Both men say that they turned the gas regulators on their FN rifles up high so that they would jam after each shot. The only men who are said to have exulted in the execution are Copeland and Boddy, both of whom were later killed and so did not survive to suggest otherwise. Whether or not Freeman and Dempster were quite so unwilling as they claim, it is certainly true that they had no real alternative but to obey orders for Callan had had the shrewdness to send with the execution party another vehicle manned by Portuguese mercenaries, and one of these sat behind a heavy machine-gun mounted in his Land Rover, watching the whole affair and providing Copeland with tacit support should he need it.

'Get running, you bastards.'

There was a brief pause, then they were all running, or rather some of them. Harry Webb and an unnamed companion walked at a leisurely pace, apparently unconcerned. Another, called Billy Brooks, advanced only a few yards, then halted, turned round, and waited for his end with arms folded. McCartney, hoping desperately for a last minute reprieve, stood on the road by the executioners, as if he was one of them.

Copeland waited until the runners had covered about thirty metres, then opened fire with his Uzi sub-machine gun. By the time he had finished his first magazine, several figures had been cut to the ground. As he fitted a second magazine, he called on the others to fire too. Freeman and Dempster, the gas regulators on their FN rifles turned up to 9, fired only one shot each before their rifles jammed. Aves and McKenzie, we are told, both aimed to miss. Only Boddy warmed to the task, shouting 'It's a turkey shoot' and exclaiming with delight when he brought down another of the running figures. Copeland expended his second magazine on those who were still running, then loaded a third and cut down the unmoving Brooks, and Harry Webb and his companion. Only McCartney was left, and as he desperately pleaded for his life Copeland fired a short burst at point-blank range into his stomach. He screamed for several seconds before Dempster (his gun now in working order), put him out of his misery with a bullet in the back of the head. The execution party then walked off down the valley to finish off the victims. Copeland killed two who had managed to survive the murderous hails of bullets, Boddy one, and Freeman, as he recalled, another: 'All the men were in agony. The one I shot had his left arm and shoulder hanging off. The right knee-cap and the bottom part of his leg was only hanging on by tendons. My rifle kept jamming because I turned the gas up on it, but Sam then pulled his machine-gun to his shoulder and pointed it at me. He gave me his pistol and said: "Shoot the man". I did so, and after that I felt very sick.'

## Callan's last throw

Whatever the feelings of Freeman and the other participants in the execution, Callan was already preoccupied with the next task—namely launching the attack on Damba which Copeland had been intending to make the night before. Some time between 18:30 and 19:00 hours that evening he set off with eighty men in eight Land Rovers. He knew from a report provided by the pilot of the Cessna that the enemy were dug in in some numbers on either side of the road which led out of Damba. It was a strong position but Callan, with the almost foolhardy bravery which characterized his military actions in Angola, had determined to attack it with a frontal assault, and trust that the element of surprise would see him through. He was not even deterred when the mission literally drove into trouble—in the form of an FNLA minefield—at the village of Quibocolo, and one of the Land Rovers blew up. Since the explosion also damaged the Land

*As news of the massacre of mercenaries came out, John Banks and other members of Security Advisory Services came under strong criticism. Here he defends himself watched by Frank Perren, one of his original partners, at a press conference (The Photo Source).*

Rover immediately behind, and since a third vehicle then had to be detailed to carry eleven casualties back to Maquela for medical treatment, Callan had to press home the attack with less than fifty men crammed into just five Land Rovers. These apparently suicidal tactics in fact proved remarkably successful. Callan later told Dempster that many of the enemy infantry immediately panicked, either running for their lives or firing randomly at friend and foe alike. Indeed the only serious resistance to the mercenaries was posed by the enemy armour. Callan himself knocked out two tanks with 66 mm rockets, and Copeland another, but a T-54 (more heavily armoured than the T-34s which the mercenaries had previously encountered) proved a very hard nut to crack. It lumbered forward in a seemingly indestructible manner and blew up one Land Rover even though the M40 guns mounted on two other Land Rovers pumped no less than nine High Explosive Anti-Tank (HEAT) shells into its body. In the end, one of the gunners, Peter, was so exasperated that he jumped down from his vehicle and resorted to a trusty 66 mm rocket, which finally did the trick. But Peter was just a fraction too late—the tank had time to fire a round into the Land Rover which happened to be carrying most of the spare ammunition. It exploded with devastating force and noise, severely wounding Peter (fractured skull) and two other mercenaries. Remarkably, these were the only casualties which occurred in the actual attack, whereas the enemy lost four tanks and an estimated 200 dead or wounded. Nevertheless, back at Maquela later that night Callan admitted to being disappointed with the level of casualties; three of the men wounded by the FNLA mine had been found to be dead on arrival at Maquela, and he just could not afford to suffer nearly twenty casualties in a single action, however successful it might have been.

The operation had, however, given Callan confidence in his more recent recruits, and the following evening—2 February—he, Copeland and 22 others set off on another mission. At first they proceeded by Land Rover, but when they were near 'Banana Junction' they abandoned their vehicles and continued their advance on foot. Satch Fortuin twisted an ankle and was left by a tree until the others should return, but the rest of the group continued for several more kilometres before taking up an ambush position on high ground overlooking the Damba road. Callan's target was again the enemy armour, so when two Land Rovers drove past he refused to allow his men to open fire on them. The following morning several lorries drove past, but again they were left unmolested. In the end, however, his patience ran out, and later that afternoon he advanced further along the edge of the road until he sighted a bulldozer which the MPLA were using as a minesweeper, three tanks and several other vehicles.

Here was the prey for which he had been waiting—the front end of an enemy column of at least twelve tanks, plus armoured cars, multi-barrelled rocket launchers, lorries, and other vehicles. Callan's killer group approached their quarry stealthily, and again the enemy were taken by surprise. Indeed the mercenaries had come to within a few yards of the column before they were spotted by a Cuban soldier who greeted them with a cry of 'Ay, Amigo'. This was their cue to open fire, which they did with such devastating effect that by the time they melted back into the bush they had destroyed all three tanks and killed (on their reckoning) some eighty men. This success merely

*A third batch of Britons flies out to Angola as mercenaries. By this time, 6 February, news of the massacre was beginning to break. Callan was missing, and the campaign virtually over (The Photo Source).*

made Callan hungry for more, and a little later he sprang another surprise further along the column; this time the results were more modest—one tank and some forty soldiers. This was followed by a third attack which accounted for three armoured cars, two trucks and another eighty or so soldiers, including some fair-haired white-skinned men whom the mercenaries assumed to be Russians. Although his men were by now emotionally and physically exhausted, Callan was determined to carry out a final attack before withdrawing. His target was the bulldozer which he had failed to damage in the first attack, but this time his luck ran out. Quite what happened is not clear, but it seems probable that during the attack Callan fired a 60 mm rocket into a lorry laden with ammunition; this blew up with tremendous force, not only devastating the MPLA/Cuban forces, but literally blowing most of the mercenaries off their feet. Two of them were seriously injured: a man known as 'Ginger' had his leg blown off, and Callan himself, who was typically leading from the front, received a leg injury which prevented him from walking. A brief fire-fight ensued in which Boddy was killed—according to Copeland, he was shot through the back of the head, though whether this was an accident or a deliberate taking of revenge by one of his fellow mercenaries is anyone's guess—but the mercenaries' primary concern now was to retreat to a place of safety. Darkness had fallen, and they travelled only a few hundred yards before collapsing for the night. There were only fifteen of them left—the rest were dead or had been separated from the main body— and this number was reduced further, first when Ginger died in the night from loss of blood, and then in the morning when two mercenaries went out on recce but never returned. With the enemy now beginning to sweep the area, the mercenaries had no option but to get moving and, carrying Callan on a makeshift stretcher, they struggled off through the bush until they came across a desolate hut. Here they decided to hole up while first Copeland and a Glaswegian called Malone, and later Christodoulou and a Portuguese mercenary called Sergeanaro, set off to try and get help from Maquela. Both Copeland and Christodoulou felt great loyalty towards the wounded Callan, and were determined to get together a party to rescue him, but not all of the others were so minded. Indeed, Dempster and a mercenary called Hussey now took the opportunity to desert, and drove off to Kinshasa in such a hurry that they left all their clothes and personal effects behind.

Meanwhile, there had been developments elsewhere of which Callan and the other mercenaries at the front were unaware. When the news of the killing of the fourteen mercenaries on Callan's orders reached Holden Roberto at Kinshasa, he flew immediately to San Antonio to tell Peter McAleese and the others based there what had happened. McAleese and a mercenary called Mick Rennie promptly flew back with Roberto to Kinshasa where they learned more details of the massacre, not least from Freeman. He, with two others, had commandeered at gunpoint a Fokker Friendship that had landed at Maquela and had forced the Portuguese pilot to fly them to Kinshasa for 'urgent medical treatment'. After a council of war, Holden Roberto and McAleese—who had by now been formally appointed Field Commander in place of Callan—accompanied by Nick Hall, Rennie, Mick Wainhouse and an American ex-policeman called Tom Oates, flew south to Maquela to bring Callan to justice. When they landed they were met by the recently arrived Christodoulou. To put him off his guard, they greeted him warmly; then McAleese suddenly attacked him violently, hitting him several times with the butt of his rifle until he collapsed on the ground.

'What were you doing shooting white mercenaries?' McAleese screamed.

'I wasn't even fucking there!' Christodoulou shouted back as best he could.

With Christodoulou under guard, the party next moved on to the base camp where they found Copeland. McAleese again extended a friendly greeting; he asked about Callan's attack, and where exactly he was holed up; a map was produced, and as Copeland bent down to the ground to show him, McAleese kicked his gun out of reach while Oates pressed the barrel of his pistol against Copeland's head.

With Copeland and Christodoulou disarmed, an instant court martial was convened. Hall, whose only experience of such proceedings was when he had been found guilty of selling arms to the Ulster Volunteer force and dishonourably discharged from the British Army, presided over the quintet. After half an hour of listening to the evidence of various witnesses, he declared Christodoulou innocent and Copeland guilty. McAleese, extraordinarily, dissented, and asked Holden Roberto, who had merely been observing, to let his old friend Copeland off. If someone had to be executed for the sake of morale, he said, let it be 'that wog' Christodoulou. Hall and Oates protested strongly at such a miscarriage of the rough justice which the court was seeking to mete out, and after some discussion Roberto confirmed Copeland's death sentence. Nevertheless, McAleese's plea is interesting, for it is clear that whatever Copeland's excesses under the leadership of Callan, he was greatly admired as a soldier. Freeman, for instance, described him as 'a great man with guns. He knew everything about them. . . He was a good guy when he came out there, but he just got into Callan's way and went round the twist.'

When McAleese's plea for Copeland failed, the latter took the only chance left to him and made a run for it, zig-zagging this way and that like a hare, desperately hoping to make it to the cover of the bush. However, the men who had been deputized to make up his execution party fired a volley of shots after him, and although he covered a lot of ground, one of them finally brought him down. Wainhouse was quickly after him, and when he reached his crumpled but still breathing body he finished him off with three bullets in the back of the head.

With Copeland dead and 'Captain' Christodoulou demoted to the rank of

Private, Callan's chances of being rescued by his fellow mercenaries had plummetted to virtually nil, yet McAleese, concerned at the prospect of him just turning up out of the bush to challenge his own authority, gave orders that he be shot on sight. In fact he never did reappear, and it was soon generally assumed by the mercenaries that he had died of his wounds.

The absence of Callan and Copeland signalled the collapse of the whole mercenary campaign. Morale had reached rock bottom, and McAleese lacked Callan's drive and military leadership. He promptly flew back to Kinshasa, and within two days Maquela had fallen without any further resistance being offered. On the Western flank the five remaining British mercenaries, now under the command of Barker, were literally caught napping in San Antonio. Too late, they realized that what they took to be another false alarm was actually the real thing. In a scene that could have been culled from a 'B' movie, they, some Angolans, and a female journalist called Robin Wright ran for a boat moored on the nearby River Congo amid a hail of small-arms fire. The majority of them made it, but Mike Johnson, an ex-Legionary, was hit in the back and killed. Barker, his military abilities and instincts coming to the fore in a crisis, did his best to organize the hasty embarkation, and then stayed on the quay to provide covering fire as the boat pulled away into the river. Barker later accused his fellow mercenaries of panicking. Either that, or he misjudged the situation. As the gap between boat and land widened fast, he threw down his rifle, stripped to his pants and dived in. But the enemy were too close. A volley of bullets ripped into the water in front of him, daring him to swim on. He stopped, turned round, and swam slowly back to the MPLA soldiers, captivity and, ultimately, the firing squad.

Meanwhile, the large military column which Callan had attacked was advancing from Maquela towards Sao Salvador. A few mercenaries were still inclined to 'give it a go' and try to stop the enemy progress, but luck had disappeared with their erstwhile leader. Christodoulou was one of nine killed, and two others were captured—the inexperienced Nammock from Kensington, and an American, Gary Acker. Shortly after these losses, McAleese ordered the remaining mercenaries to withdraw from Sao Salvador, and that, apparently, was that.

Or rather it would have been had not the Angolans, urged on by their Cuban advisors, decided to put on trial thirteen captured mercenaries. It was to be a show trial, to reveal to the world the crime of mercenarism—and the prize exhibit was to be none other than Callan. He had been captured after about two weeks in the bush, along with five other mercenaries. They had loyally stood by him and had carried him on a stretcher in a vain attempt to reach safety. In the end, however, starvation, dehydration and exhaustion had caught up with them, so that when they were finally captured it came as a relief to their desperate condition (see Chapter 6 for Colin Evans'

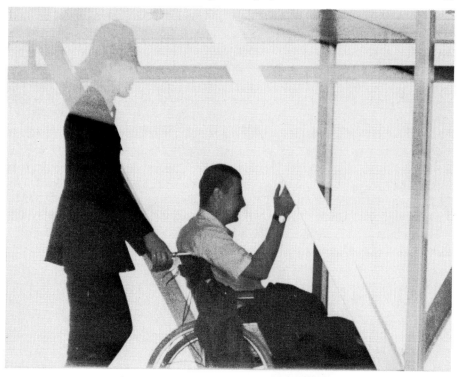

**Above** *An injured mercenary returns home, wiser and not much richer for the experience* (The Photo Source).

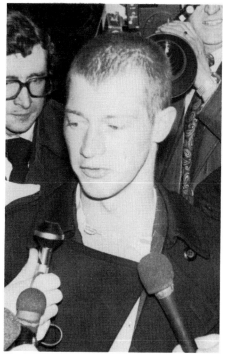

**Right** *The press, having given Banks and his fellow recruiters much free and willing advertising, now throng greedily round a shocked young mercenary Andrew Black, who went to Angola as a flying instructor and returned with a tale of Callan's massacre* (The Photo Source).

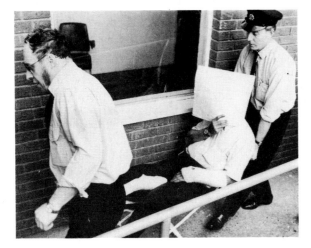

*A mercenary comes back from the war — in plaster and anxious to avoid publicity (Associated Press).*

personal account of this time in the bush and consequent imprisonment).

The trial of the thirteen mercenaries—nine Britons and four Americans—began on 11 June. The prosecution and defence put their cases—all the mercenaries were called upon to give evidence—in less than a fortnight and amidst an enormous blaze of publicity. It was, of course, a show trial. The prosecutor, Rui Monteiro, urged that the trial should be used to teach the western powers a lesson, and he demanded the death penalty for ideological reasons.

'Comrades, pioneers, in your name, in the name of all pioneers fallen, in the name of all the people of the world assassinated by the guns, machine-guns, fire shells, fragmentation shells, beatings and hangings of imperialism, in your name I ask for the death penalty.'

The prisoner on whom eyes were most firmly fixed during the trial was, inevitably, Callan, but when his turn came to give evidence he singularly failed to satisfy the desires of the vultures. 'All I want to say is this. All my men were under my command, and any charges against them . . . OK . . . they were following orders. I don't want to answer any more questions. No disrespect.' Later, however, on 20 June he made a longer speech. Observers found it confused, though the main bones of it were clear enough. 'I am responsible. I gave the order for the execution. No one else . . . I am afraid of the prison. No wants to die but I am prepared to die.' It is clear from what his fellow prisoner Colin Evans told me that he was not merely confused by this stage, but mentally ill. Evans says that Callan was 'potty' and a 'fruit and nut case', and describes how Callan was living in a fantasy world, often shouting out orders from his cell as if in charge of troops on the battlefield, and calling for help on a non-existent military radio.

Whatever Callan's fitness to stand trial, however, on 28 June the court pronounced its verdict. All thirteen men were found guilty, and of these four

were condemned to death: Callan, Andrew McKenzie, John 'Brummie' Barker and the American Daniel Gearhart, who had once offered his services in the American magazine *Soldier of Fortune*. The nine others were given long prison sentences, varying from sixteen to thirty years. The death sentences came as a real shock, though not perhaps as a total surprise. Immediately

**Above and right** *Three views of Callan on trial for his life — taking advice from his defence attorney, walking forward to give evidence and deep in thought. He fully accepted responsibility for the actions of all his men, yet it is clear from what he said, and from what Colin Evans has told the author, that Callan was mentally unfit for trial* (GAMMA/Spooner, Rex Features).

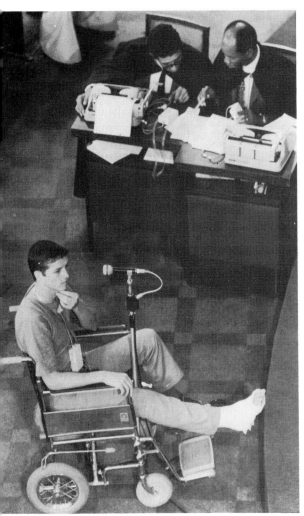

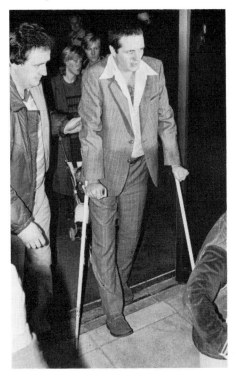

**Left** *John Nammock, with an injured leg, pleads before the Angolan court* (GAMMA /Spooner).

**Above** *Nammock received a 16-year sentence, but limped back into Heathrow nearly eight years later* (Popperfoto).

there were appeals for clemency, from Queen Elizabeth II and the Prime Minister of Britain, and also from the President of the United States of America. Inside the prison the condemned men still hoped for—indeed almost expected—a reprieve, but President Neto was determined to make an example of the quartet. On Saturday 10 July, after a meeting with the British Ambassador at which they wrote final letters to their families at home, they were taken to a place called Revolutionary Field outside Luanda and shot.

For the remainder, years of imprisonment lay ahead. The three Americans were released in December 1982, but the Britons had to wait until March 1984 before they too were put on a plane and flown home, in a final brief burst of publicity. After that, it was a question of trying to pick up the threads of their broken lives.

*Mike Hoare, the most famous mercenary of modern times and founder of 5 Commando (Camera Press).*

*Mike Hoare's men in action in the Congo (Camera Press).*

**Left** *A German mercenary in the Congo (Camera Press).*

**Right** *Col Jean Schramme who led 10 Commando in the mercenary revolt in the Congo in 1967 after Hoare's departure (Camera Press).*

**Far right** *A Katangese soldier, well-equipped for action (Camera Press).*

**Right** *A nonchalant-looking mercenary in the Congo (Camera Press).*

**Left** *MPLA soldiers load a 'Stalin's Organs' rocket launcher in Angola (GAMMA/Spooner).*

**Above** *Thirteen mercenaries on trial in Angola, with the whole world as witness, courtesy of newspapers and television* (Sipa/Rex).

**Below** *Some of the thirteen mercenaries on trial in Angola. Nammock and Wiseman are nearest to the camera. The notorious Callan is in the centre with black hair, and beyond him is a thin, puzzled Colin Evans* (Sipa/Rex).

**Above** *Southern Angola. Though the short-lived campaign by British mercenaries in Northern Angola grabbed the headlines, in the south the MPLA forces were faced by a more resolute foe, UNITA, whose efforts at that time and since have been less newsworthy, but more significant. They are led by Jonas Savimbi, seen here surrounded by some of his men* (The Photo Source).

**Below** *UNITA troops advance through the undergrowth* (The Photo Source).

**Left** *Chinese weapons captured from UNITA being put on display by the MPLA (The Photo Source).*

**Right** *UNITA soldiers on parade in a camp in southeast Angola (The Photo Source).*

**Left** *Two South African soldiers assisting UNITA are among the group of prisoners pictured here. UNITA continues to receive help from the South Africans, as well as from individual mercenaries (The Photo Source).*

## Chapter 3

# Seychelles—Mike Hoare's finale

At 09:00 hours on Wednesday, 25 November 1981, the 65-seat Fokker F-28 which comprised the whole of the Royal Swazi Airline's fleet took off from Manzini in Swaziland and headed off across the Indian Ocean bound for the holiday islands of the Seychelles. With one passenger having failed to check in, there were 48 passengers on board. These included just two women, and both disembarked at the Comores Islands, the one scheduled stop on the journey to an earthly paradise. The plane continued on its way, and, at 17:30 hours local time, after a journey without incident, it landed at the international airport on Mahé, the main island of the Seychelles. The plane taxied to a halt, mobile steps were brought to the side of the plane, and within a few minutes all the remaining passengers—tired after a long journey, and also markedly tense—had disgorged on to the tarmac.

They were a remarkably fit and tough-looking bunch. But then this was not surprising since they were, they said, all members of the Ancient Order of Frothblowers, a rugby club whose players had come to the picturesque Seychelles to soak up sun, drink and the good life. Two men stood out from the rest, not least because of their age. They were, of course, the managers—one tall, grey haired, with moustache and sideburns, the other a tidy, dapper figure, well dressed with a goatee beard. That, at least, was the story. But it was not, of course, the truth. In reality, the two older men were none other than Gerry Puren and Mike Hoare, veterans of the Congo, while the 44 'rugby players' who accompanied them were in truth mercenaries with rifles stowed away in their baggage. And their mission was to overthrow the government of the Seychelles.

## The plan

Five years previously, on 29 June 1976, the islands of the Seychelles had embraced independence. Leading the celebrations on that occasion was the flamboyant first President, Jimmy Mancham, friend of the famous and a man with a distinct penchant for women of the international jet set. One year later, however, he had been deposed—like many another leader before and since while he was attending a Commonwealth conference in London. The coup was almost bloodless: there was no Seychelles army to deal with, and

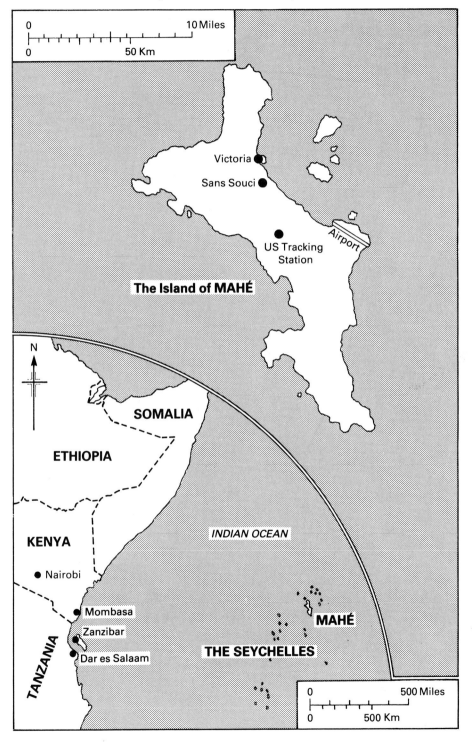

0     10 Miles

0     50 Km

Victoria

Sans Souci

Airport

US Tracking
Station

**The Island of MAHÉ**

N

**SOMALIA**

**ETHIOPIA**

**KENYA**

● Nairobi

**TANZANIA**

● Mombasa
● Zanzibar
● Dar es Salaam

*INDIAN OCEAN*

**MAHÉ**

**THE SEYCHELLES**

0     500 Miles

0     500 Km

*The unconvincing Seychelles militia, established by President René and pictured here on the anniversary of his coming to power* (Camera Press).

the police force was small, so once its armoury had been seized, there was little it could do about it.

The new president was the man who had been Mancham's Prime Minister, France-Albert René. Though both Mancham and René had trained as barristers in London, they were men of very different stamps. René was a radical socialist, whereas Mancham was a playboy conservative. René had pressed hard for independence, whereas Mancham had vigorously opposed it. Yet, ironically, it was Mancham who had got the people's vote when independence came. However, his style of life and government did not endear him to everyone, and especially not to René and the Seychelles People's United Party. And so they carried out their coup.

René immediately set about instigating his socialist programme of change: money was poured into education, health, the social services—and the army. The latter was an important new development, for although it was never intended to be very large—500 or 600 men, trained by Tanzanians provided by President Nyerere—it was instituted above all to ensure that no-one else could ever imitate René's almost peaceful seizure of power. If Mancham wanted to regain his former position of strength, he would have to use force.

Mancham took up exile in Putney, London, there pursuing the good life and plotting his return, though the man who took it upon himself to pursue that eventuality most actively was Mike Hoare. An accountant by profession, but not by inclination, Hoare was a man who thrived on adventure, and the idea of a mercenary comeback clearly appealed to him a lot. In addition he had strong emotional attachments to the Seychelles, where he had spent many of his happiest moments, and he was, of course, strongly right wing and anti-communist. It is no surprise, then, to find that before long he was drawing up proposals to initiate a coup which would depose René and return Mancham. Indeed, as early as May 1978 he was writing to one of Mancham's inner circle concerning 'Plan No 2'. Although the brief letter vouchsafes no details, the fact that the plan was one to carry out a mercenary coup in the Seychelles is confirmed by the postscript: 'Beware of a man named Banks in Britain. He is very dangerous and bad news in our line of country.'

That it took so long for Hoare's plans to reach fruition was due to a variety of matters, not least the lack of money. Whereas Hoare felt that some $5 million would be required to guarantee success, in the event he was forced to settle for something less than half a million, and tailor his plans accordingly. George Schroeder, himself a veteran of the Congo, was later to tell the Press that he had turned down the opportunity to join in Hoare's operation because it was not soundly based, and he also stated that he had informed the South African government about it. But it is clear now not only that the plan was in fact very carefully thought out, but also that the South African security services were in close touch with Hoare from early on in the proceedings.

Hoare was not a man to be slipshod, and that he twice personally reconnoitred the Seychelles prior to the attempted coup was revealed by the Seychellois authorities when they displayed his captured passport shortly afterwards. In order to hide his identity, he had doctored his passport, changing the 'H' of his name to a 'B', and adding an 'l' to the end. However, closer inspection of the document and his passport photograph revealed the fact that 'Mr Boarel' was none other than 'Mad Mike'. Visa stamps showed that he had visited the islands in both June and September. The former was particularly significant for it coincided with the anniversary of President René's accession to power, when a parade of the might of his tiny army would have revealed to the watching Hoare and his companion Tullio Moneta what they would be up against.

Furthermore, as Anthony Mockler has described in detail in his book *The New Mercenaries*, Hoare received the active help of the South African military intelligence service. They provided him with weapons and equip-ment—automatic rifles, rocket-launchers, hand grenades, ammunition, radios—and also helped him to finalize his plans. A key matter was getting the arms into the Seychelles. At first it was decided that they should be taken in separately by boat in advance of the mercenaries, who would fly in under the cover of being tourists. However, this plan had to be abandoned when Brigadier Hammam of military intelligence warned Hoare off the idea as being too risky. At first, too, Major Willie Ward of the 1st Recce Regiment offered to use his influence to raise a 'mercenary' force for Hoare, but a month before the operation was due he pulled out, leaving Hoare in the lurch. Hoare had no intention of giving up at this stage, and before long he had assembled a group of just over fifty men to carry out his plans—a mixture of veterans of the Congo, members of the Recce Commandos and men who had served in the Rhodesian special forces.

The motives of these men were the usual mixture of a desire for a bit of adventure and the expectation of making some easy money. Not that they would necessarily admit as such. Martin Dolinchek, for instance, claimed later that he became involved because he had been told that 'the Seychelles is a Communist tyranny run by Soviets and Marxists and the Libyan regime', but much more honest and revealing are the words of Aubrey Brooks who, when he faced the Press following his capture, couldn't even recall the name of the man they had been trying to reinstate: 'I received $1,000 down payment and never met any person who paid us. But I believe it was done on behalf of the former President. Mongon? Montson? I am not sure of his name.' As for Johan Fritz, the one mercenary to be killed in the operation, and scion of a wealthy Johannesburg family, he was later said by a friend to have become bored by a life of 'suburban tea and tennis' after he had served a period of national service in the Parachute Battalion. That description strikes much nearer the truth, although it must also be acknowledged that the fact that the mercenaries saw the operation as being in South Africa's interests may have helped to persuade some of them that it was an adventure worth pursuing. But it was certainly not a motivating force.

By the time that Hoare flew into Mahé international airport with the main group of mercenaries on 25 November, there were already a total of nine others already on the island. They had entered in dribs and drabs over the previous month, to check on the lie of the land and make preparations. They included Bob Sims, Hoare's brother-in-law, his lover Sue Ingle, and the maverick figure of Martin Dolinchek, an operative of the South African National Intelligence Service who later claimed that he had taken an extended period of leave in order to go on the mission. With the exception of Sue Ingle, each member of the party had entered the Seychelles carrying a cricket bag, in the bottom of which, beneath a false bottom, was an automatic rifle. From Hoare's point of view, this was a way of testing out airport security, for he had decided that, since shipping arms in was now considered too risky, then the only way to take them in was concealed in the luggage of each mercenary. This might have been ridiculously risky at many airports, but security in the Seychelles was much less stringent, and when all eight males managed to carry their weapons through customs without a hitch, this confirmed Hoare's opinion that there was no good reason why the rest of them should not do so without being detected.

This change of plan was, however, something that he was careful to keep to himself, and it was not until the early hours of the 25th, the day on which they were to fly in, that Hoare told his bleary-eyed men that they would be taking their own weaponry with them. They were, initially, aghast, but at this late stage only one man was prepared to use it as an excuse to back out of the operation. The rest were too unwilling to lose face.

## The operation

At first, things went absolutely according to plan. The air trip was uneventful, the Fokker F-28 arrived at Mahé airport right on time, and the arrival of the 46-strong Ye Ancient Order of Frothblowers gave rise to no surprise or suspicion amongst the airport officials. 'Mr Boarel', looking every inch the part of an efficient sports team manager in his blazer, tie and slacks, with a monocle in his breast pocket, led the way to passport control. One by one their passports were checked and stamped. The men then proceeded to pick up their luggage, walk through the 'nothing to declare' channel of

*The distinguished and dapper Mike Hoare, or 'Mr Boarel' as his doctored passport declared (Camera Press).*

customs, and out of the small terminal to be met by the advance party, who were ready and waiting with three minibuses to take them to their hotel. The anxiety of the previous weeks must have seemed to Hoare rather absurd—getting three rugby teams of armed mercenaries through the Seychelles passport control and customs was, it seemed, child's play. But disaster, in an unexpected and almost ridiculous form, lay in wait.

Kevin Beck was one of the last men off the plane. He followed his comrades through passport control, collected his bag, and then, incredibly, walked through the 'something to declare' channel of customs. Why he did so is unclear—perhaps a mixture of drink, tiredness, elation, and sheer carelessness—but that, unquestionably and disastrously, is what he did. Although he protested that he had nothing to declare, the customs officer, not surprisingly, insisted on searching his bag. At the bottom, he felt what he realized was a weapon and promptly asked Beck to come through to an inner room. There, a policewoman and male Sergeant took over. At first, the former assumed the weapon to be nothing more lethal than a speargun for undersea hunting—which would have to be impounded until Beck left the island. But the Sergeant realized that it was something a lot more dangerous. He asked Beck what it was. Beck denied that he had ever seen it before. He then added, with a crassness that almost defies belief, that there were another 44 men outside with identical bags. With that, the game was well and truly up.

The Sergeant ran out of the building towards the minibuses, shouting to raise the alarm, but Puren, quick to react to the hitch, had his rifle in his hands and fired two shots into the Sergeant's shoulder. Pandemonium broke out, compounded by the fact that the light of day was rapidly giving way to the dark of night. Amidst the confusion and shooting, one mercenary, Johan Fritz, was shot and killed—by one of his fellow mercenaries. The first priority for Hoare and his men was to round up all the airport staff, but with their cover blown he knew that it could only be a matter of time before the Seychellois military, assisted by their Tanzanian 'advisers', and police moved

The Fokker-28 in which the mercenaries flew into Mahé airport in the Seychelles. Note the shell holes in the fuselage (Popperfoto).

into action. In such situations, a quick decision is essential, and Hoare made his, sending four of the advance party, followed after a short interval by a minibus load of others, to attack and take control of the nearby barracks. It was, perhaps, an overoptimistic mission for so few men—and the effect was comparable to the time, on his first campaign in the Congo, when he sent men to 'investigate' a lighted building near Albertville airport; they provoked such a hornet's nest reaction that he was forced to beat a very hasty retreat. Of the four men who first attacked the barracks, two were wounded—one in the arm, one in the thigh—and by the time their support arrived it was clear that 'securing' the barracks was going to be anything but a pushover. So the mercenaries retreated, and the Seychellois began a counter-attack, with jeeps and an armoured car which, invulnerable to the bullets of the mercenaries' automatics (they had been unable to carry anything more lethal through customs) threatened to prove a decisive factor. In the end, however, it immobilized itself by getting wedged in a rut. The mercenaries were then able to surround it and force its occupants to surrender. Mockler believes that they did so by the ruthless expedient of threatening to pour petrol down the barrel and then ignite it; when the officer inside refused to bow to this pressure, he was, Mockler believes, shot by one of his own men who had no intention of being burnt alive inside a metal box.

The consequence of the capture of the armoured car was that the rest of the Seychellois troops retreated, allowing an uneasy peace to descend on the benighted airport. But despite their success, the thoughts of a number of the mercenaries were now turning not towards capitalizing on it, but to escaping. Hoare and his old Congo mercenaries were by and large of the opinion that all was not lost, and that the coup could still be successfully carried out, but the others disagreed. The prospect of being stuck in the Seychelles, surrounded by their enemies and with no means of escape, was not one which they relished. The only obvious way out was on the plane that had brought them in, but when Puren rang the pilots up at the hotel to which they had gone, they told him they were not interested in extricating them. It seemed, therefore, that there was no option but to fight on. The only way out was to carry through the coup attempt successfully.

If the mercenaries' best laid plans had been undone by a visitation of Nemesis—in the form of Kevin Beck—in the best traditions of Greek tragedy a 'deus ex machina' intervention was fast approaching, some 40,000 feet above the Indian Ocean. The only other plane due to land in the Seychelles that night was an Air India jet piloted by Captain Umesh Saxena, en route from Salisbury to Bombay. In accordance with normal procedures, Saxena radioed in to Mahé international airport to confirm his approach and ask permission to land, but he could, at first, raise no reply. He tried again and again, but without success, and finally announced over the intercom to his passengers that he was going to have to divert to Mauritius. Almost immediately, however, a 'not too professional' voice broke in over his radio, and gave him permission to land at Mahé. So he countermanded his announcement, and continued on his course to the Seychelles.

The reason why Saxena had been unable to establish contact with Mahé control tower was simple enough. The only person in it at that time was hiding under the table with a dustbin lid over his head! After the mercenaries' cover had been broken and the shooting had started, the airport staff had quickly been rounded up. Included amongst the prisoners were the three women operating the control tower. Later, however, Charles Goatley and two other mercenaries had taken the Director of Civil Aviation for the airport to the control tower since they had been informed that an Air India flight was due in later that evening. While they were there, however, the Seychellois had launched their counter-attack. The Director, Mr Lousteau-Lalanne, later described in court what happened next. 'The armed men noticed the lights of two vehicles approaching the runway. They became quite agitated. Eventually there was an exchange of fire, and the armed men fled from the tower. For my own safety I had to crawl under the desk and place a metal dustbin over my head.' And there Mr Lousteau-Lalanne remained until the mercenaries returned. He was too frightened to move, and although Saxena tried several times to make contact, he made no attempt to reply. When Goatley returned, however, and realized what was happening, he himself made contact with Saxena and in his 'not too professional' voice gave him permission to land despite the wretched Director's protests.

Landing was no straightforward matter, however, for three vehicles had been abandoned on the runway and had not been cleared. They now presented themselves as potentially lethal obstacles to the incoming aircraft. Saxena managed to miss two of them, but he clipped the third with the tip of his port wing, though not hard enough to cause any significant damage. Soon after he had halted, he and his pilot were escorted off the plane to meet Hoare, and not long afterwards the Seychellois opened fire again. This immediately put Hoare in a quandary. He himself was keen to press on with the coup, but the airliner's arrival put him in a spot. If a stray Seychellois shell were to hit the airliner, the death of any passenger would unquestionably be blamed on him. He therefore got one of his colleagues to phone the Commissioner of Police and, after some negotiation, managed to get the Seychellois to stop shelling until the airliner took off. He was told, however, that the mercenaries must not fly out on the plane, and he himself must stay in telephone contact to ensure that this was the case.

In the meantime, while the shelling and small-arms fire was still continuing, there was considerable tension on the plane. 'It was', one of the passengers confirmed, 'very nerve-wracking. For ten minutes we sat in the darkness listening to the sound of automatic fire and watching the tracers.' Three mercenaries who had boarded the plane tried to keep them calm. 'They told us we had landed at a very unfortunate time, and politely asked us to be patient and not to panic.'

But if Hoare was keen to get the airliner and its passengers out of the way so that he could continue his mission, the majority of the mercenaries saw things differently. They saw the airliner as a route to safety. They had lost their appetite for a fight against even as small and inexperienced an army as the Seychellois one, and in the end it was the majority view that prevailed, much to the disgust of some of the Congo veterans. Hoare himself was very reluctant to pull out at this stage, and wanted to stay in the Seychelles and see what he could do, but his men were anxious that he accompany them, not least because they felt he would be useful in negotiations with the South African authorities. When Kurt Priefert and Tullio Moneta made it clear that they were prepared to use force if necessary, Hoare agreed to 'come quietly' and board the airliner.

So, despite the agreement which Hoare had made, the mercenaries trooped on board the Air India jet, still carrying their automatics, and sank into the vacant seats, 'Looking tired but cheerful' according to one passenger. The hijack of the plane—the mercenaries insisted on the word 'hijack' not being used however—was almost gentlemanly. Saxena, who had no option, agreed to fly them out, and once they were airborne everyone on board was remarkably chummy. One of the air hostesses recalled: 'We served them

*The Air India jet which was hijacked by Mike Hoare's mercenaries and flew them out of the 'frying pan' of the Seychelles to an international 'fire' in South Africa (Camera Press).*

drinks and what food we had left. They were so polite and gentlemanly that it just did not seem as if we were being hijacked.' One passenger at least, a Mr Benning, seemed to enjoy the unusual experience: 'We had a few beers together with the men. They were very friendly. The atmosphere was a bit like that after a good rugby match.'

But if drink helped the mercenaries to forget their troubles for a few hours, reality awaited them at Louis Botha Airport, Durban, where they touched down shortly before 05:00 hours. There, prolonged negotiations with various South African authorities took place before the mercenaries were handcuffed and taken off to Zonderwater Prison near Cullinan.

## The aftermath

Almost immediately the allegations and counter-allegations began to fly thick and fast over two issues: the attempted coup and the actual hijack. The South African Foreign Minister stated that it was common knowledge that two dissident groups of Seychellois exiles existed. He said that representatives of these groups had approached the government 'several times', but insisted that 'on each and every occasion their representatives were told categorically that it was the policy of the South African government not to involve itself with adventures of this nature'. The hijack was played down, and despite international calls for the mercenaries to be punished, on 2 December the South African authorities unconditionally freed 39 of the 44 hijackers, and

*Peter Duffy, one of the mercenaries who hoped to overthrow the regime of President René. He is pictured here after his initial release by the South African authorities, but was later re-arrested and tried (Camera Press).*

allowed the remaining five, who included Mike Hoare, to be released on bail on a provisional charge of kidnapping.

This move, designed to prevent any in-depth investigation of the affair, brought an immediate response from, amongst others, Kurt Waldheim, the Secretary General of the United Nations. He stated that 'the action of the South African government cannot but encourage those who contemplate such grossly illegal actions as hijacking and the reprehensible use of mercenaries'. The criticism was not merely from outside South Africa. In the South African parliament, the chief whip of the Progressive Federal Party, Brian Bamford, called the release of the mercenaries 'scandalous', and he said that it would 'add fuel to the suspicions that people have voiced overseas about South African alleged involvement'. But to have taken the course which Bamford wanted would not merely have added fuel but actually have confirmed suspicions.

The Minister of Police, Louis le Grange, preferred a different tack. He claimed that the mercenaries had broken no law, and he played down the fighting which had taken place in the Seychelles. All the mercenaries had done, he claimed, was 'to shoot out a few windows and run around in the bush', a description which conveniently ignored the fact that two men were killed in the fighting and a number of others injured.

The following day, 7 December, the protestations that the South African government had not been in any way involved began to look decidedly unconvincing when the Seychelles authorities displayed the captured Martin Dolinchek to the press, revealing him to be, as he admitted, an officer of the National Intelligence Service. Throughout the rest of the month the pressure began to build up from both within and without South Africa until, on 1 January, the Attorney General authorized the arrest of all the mercenaries. They were to stand trial on the charge of having transgressed the National Aviation Act. There was no question of them being charged for being mercenaries as such since mercenarism was not a crime.

When, however, in early February, a United Nations commission arrived in South Africa to investigate the abortive coup attempt, it encountered an official wall of non-co-operation, and was forced to return to New York after having been denied the opportunity speak to the mercenaries. Carlos Ozores of Panama, the leader of the commission, complained that 'anywhere else in the world we would have access to these men. We wanted to ask about the coup and not about the hijacking.' Of course, the South African authorities had no desire that anyone, least of all an independent group of outsiders, should dig below the surface of the affair, but in the end it was impossible to keep matters hidden. This was firstly because in the Seychelles, where the other seven mercenaries had been captured, Martin Dolinchek was proving a severe embarrassment to the National Intelligence Service. The second reason was that, with Hoare and the others on trial in South Africa, it was almost inevitable that Hoare's dealings with the National Intelligence Service and with officers of military intelligence would come to the surface.

The trial of the 46 men who escaped back to South Africa lasted from 10 March to 30 July 1982. On 12 March, a clear hint that members of the government, as well as of the intelligence services, were more implicated in the affair than they were willing to admit was provided by the evidence of Lieutenant Colonel Jacob Monta who asserted that when the mercenaries landed at the Louis Botha Airport, Durban, one of their leaders, Peter Duffy (a Congo veteran, and a photographer) told him: 'This is a very serious case. . .there are seven or eight members of the government involved'. It was perhaps with this in mind that on 15 March the judge ordered the court to be cleared and said that the case should continue for the time being in secret. This would, he said, enable the defence 'to put their cards on the table'. He had been persuaded that it was in the interests of the state that certain evidence should be held in camera. But if government members were not directly implicated in open court, members of the intelligence services were. Hoare himself gave evidence, and told of meetings with both the Deputy Director of the National Intelligence Service, N.J. Claasen, and with two Brigadiers from military intelligence, who also provided him with arms. He also insisted that the government too was 'fully aware' of the plans for the coup, but failed to provide chapter and verse.

*A drawn Mike Hoare arrives at Pietermaritzburg Supreme Court to hear its verdict. He received ten years, but served less than four (Popperfoto).*

In the end the mercenaries were found guilty, as was inevitable, but the sentences were, for the most part, more in the way of a light smack on the hand than anything else. All were found guilty of endangering the Air India jet and its occupants, and for that they received six months. Only seven of them, however, were found guilty of what was effectively a charge of hijacking, and it was Hoare who received by far the stiffest sentence—ten years plus another ten years suspended. The others received between one and five years. That is not to say, however, that they all served a full sentence. With remission, the majority were freed after just four months, and Hoare himself was released in May 1985 after having served a sentence which the authorities perhaps deemed to have been sufficient—both as a punishment to him for failing in his attempt, and as a sop to world opinion.

Was the eventual punishment just? That is perhaps an unanswerable question. What has to be kept in mind is that the mercenaries were punished not for being mercenaries, nor for causing damage, injury or death in the Seychelles, but for commandeering an Air India jet which they had lured into a dangerous situation. World opinion was disturbed too by the actual coup attempt and the apparent involvement of the South African intelligence services, and perhaps government members too, in a mercenary venture. That could not be entirely ignored. So Hoare received a stiff sentence, and was severely chastized by the Press. He was described as a 'man of no scruple', and his Congo exploits were attacked although they were strictly irrelevant to the present case. (Mr Justice Neville described them as exploits 'which newspaper reporters at the time recall as having had as much to do with pillage and looting as the heroic rescue of white civilians from the rampaging Congolese soldiery'.) Such words seem to me to be more in the way of satisfying world opinion than anything else. They should not, however, be allowed to obscure the fact that Neville, although he stated that it was clear that 'certain members' of the South African defence forces had 'lent aid and support' to the coup, also absolved the army and its high command from official involvement. Such absolution may have been correct. But both Hoare and Duffy seem to have genuinely believed that knowledge of the coup—and tacit approval of it—stretched up into the higher echelons of government. If so, they must have felt bitter about their sentences. In the end, however, when Hoare had been forgotten by the world and the Press had long since moved on to fresher stories, he was quietly released, and promptly announced that most of what had been written about the affair was rubbish. He would, he said, write his own account of what really happened.

Meanwhile, in the Seychelles, all the mercenaries who had not flown out on the Air India jet had undergone their own ordeal. Six of them had been rounded up quickly but Gerry Puren had spent two weeks in hiding before he gave himself up at a police station, hungry and still clad in the same clothes in which he had come to the country. All seven were originally charged with treason. However, charges against the single female, Sue Ingle, were dropped and she was discreetly whisked out of the country. The charge of treason against her companion-cum-lover, Bob Sims, was also dropped, but he still stood accused of illegally bringing weapons into the country. The five others, however, were faced with the grim prospect that if they were found guilty of the charge of treason they were liable to the ultimate penalty—death. It therefore came as something of a shock to onlookers and members of the court when four of these men, on the advance of their lawyer Nicholas Fairbairn, pleaded guilty. This was not the result of some mental aberration or suicidal intention, but a move designed to take the wind out of the judge's sails. If they all pleaded guilty, and if the evidence against them was therefore not paraded before the Press and public, it would appear an act of remarkable vengefulness if they were then condemned to death. Fairbairn seems to have decided that there was little chance of securing a verdict of not guilty, and so the best move was to try and obtain a sentence of imprisonment rather than death.

The fifth man, Martin Dolinchek, had, however, decided to defend himself. He entered a confused plea which the judge interpreted as being one of 'not guilty', and so the trial continued, with the details of the whole affair therefore being made public. Dolinchek achieved by such means a sentence of twenty years' imprisonment for himself, but the others—Aubrey Brooks, Gerry Puren, Roger England and Barney Carey—were all sentenced to death by hanging. In the event, however, they were more fortunate than the quartet of Angolan mercenaries who were condemned to death. After, at President René's request, sacking Fairbairn and withdrawing an appeal, they were reprieved from the gallows. Indeed later, after refusing to get embroiled in an army mutiny, they were transferred from their cells to much more pleasant conditions on a small island, where life was at least relatively comfortable.

*Aubrey Brooks (left) and Roger England are put on public display after their capture in the Seychelles. Both were later sentenced to death, but granted a reprieve (Associated Press).*

And so the affair ended. A coup planned with some skill, and condemned to failure by a few moments of almost incomprehensible behaviour. A coup which provoked, remarkably, two trials. A coup which stands as a classic case of mercenary activity being conducted with considerable assistance from intelligence services—and with the tacit approval of who knows who else. But a coup which ultimately altered little and which proved, amongst other things, that the greatest crime a mercenary can commit is to fail.

Chapter 4

# A worldwide phenomenon

The three previous chapters have concentrated on what are probably the three most famous—or notorious—mercenary operations of recent times. They are not entirely typical of modern mercenary activity, yet at the same time each stands out as a classic example of its type.

Mike Hoare's three consecutive campaigns in the Congo are outstanding as an example of a sustained, successful period of campaigning by freelance mercenaries. I use the word 'sustained' with some caution, however. Although Hoare remained the commanding officer of 5 Commando during that period, the membership of the unit was far from static. The contracts signed by the mercenaries were for six months at a time, and although they were renewable, few men were inclined to take up the option. Thus few men who served in the first six-month period signed on for the second one, and although a number of old hands did come back for the third period, the majority of the soldiers then were again newcomers.

Nor should it be forgotten that Hoare's success was not merely down to the skill and bravery of himself and his men; as he himself admitted, much depended on air superiority, and in particular the mercenary Cuban pilots who flew the planes. Without such support, Hoare's success would have been much less. Nevertheless, it is also true that his own leadership was very important to the emergence of 5 Commando as a crucial fighting unit. He certainly had the ability to inspire his men, as one of his Sergeants, Robin Griffin, testified. He recalled how, on one of the many occasions on which the front of the mobile column was ambushed, Hoare was disgusted by the fact that all the men around him, although they were a hundred yards or so back from the ambush, threw themselves into the ditches on either side of the road and stayed there, taking cover. While one of his officers went forward to check out the situation, he himself 'ordered his driver to get his map table and chair out, and set them up in the middle of the road. He then sat down and started studying the maps as we sheepishly started crawling out of the ditches.' It was, as Griffin said, 'pure ham on his part, but by God it was impressive, and good for morale'.

Hoare's skill at leadership also came through during the periods of unrest which periodically broke out when his men lost patience with waiting for their pay. On one occasion his men refused to go on parade, but Hoare refused to talk to them about the pay problem until they did go on parade. It was a stand-off situation, but after a few hours the men did fall in. Griffin recalled how Hoare at first 'went through his inspection routine, crapped on some of us about haircuts and not shaving, then gathered us around informally and told us that he couldn't guarantee we would get paid, but he would do everything in his power to see we were. Those who wanted to fight on that basis could stay on, the rest could go back to Johannesburg with no hard feelings.' The consequence of this was that only twenty men left, over 200 stayed on, and before long the pay came through. At the same time, Hoare was not infallible. The way in which he refused to abort his very first campaign, against Albertville, despite the fact that almost everything seemed to be against it—he expected 100 men and ended up going with fewer than twenty, the radios failed to arrive, one of his boats was sabotaged during transit, and morale amongst his untrained troops was bad—says much for his determination but little for his powers of judgement. In the final analysis, however, Hoare was successful—and it is by the criterion of winning and losing that any military leader has ultimately to be judged.

What Hoare's exploits in the Congo seemed to prove was that a few white men, decently armed and decently clad, could change the course of African history. Independence might be coming to the continent, but professional white soldiers would continue to dominate military events wherever they were found. Such a view had soon to be revised, however. When, in 1967, the south-eastern sector of Nigeria broke away under the leadership of Colonel Ojukwu and declared itself the independent state of Biafra, the consequence was a bloody war that lasted until 1970. It soon attracted the attention of Congo veterans and other would-be mercenaries, but it became clear as events unrolled that Biafra was going to be no repeat of the Congo. Although some of the mercenaries who were hired by Ojukwu did perform almost heroically, the majority did not. For the latter, it was more a case of take the money and run, once it became clear that fighting in Biafra was going to be no picnic.

Thus towards the end of 1967 Robert Faulques, formerly of the 1$^{er}$ REP of the French Foreign Legion, signed a contract with Ojukwu which committed him to find a force of 100 mercenaries to come to Biafra and train and lead his Biafran troops. In the event, however, Faulques assembled only fifty-odd men, and then flew off to Paris to buy arms and equipment. In his absence, the majority of the mercenaries, rather than concentrating on the training duties for which they had been hired, decided to mount an attack on a Nigerian position at Calabar. They seem to have expected an easy victory, but received a sharp lesson in the realities of warfare in Nigeria when they were forced to withdraw leaving behind five of their comrades dead. When Faulques returned from Paris, he promptly wound up the operation, and he

and most of his men left Biafra for good, somewhat wiser and also—since they had received six months' pay in advance—substantially better off than they had a right to expect. Faulques, indeed, seems to have pocketed the advance pay for the forty-odd men whom he never actually hired.

A few mercenaries did stay behind to fulfil their obligations, however, most notably a German called Rolf Steiner and a Welshman known as Taffy Williams. The former, like Faulques, had served in the 1er REP, and he now set about reforming the Fourth Commando Brigade, a force of Biafrans under the command of a handful of mercenaries. He did not, again like Faulques, have much desire to get closely involved in the fighting, and it was Williams who took the leading part in the field. Williams was one of the few mercenaries to leave Biafra with his reputation enhanced. He made a deep impression on those who came into contact with him, not least the journalist—and future bestseller writer—Frederick Forsyth. Williams, it is interesting to note, had a very low opinion of his fellow mercenaries—Forsyth describes it as 'unprintable'—but a very high one of the Biafrans alongside whom he fought. 'I've seen a lot of Africans at war, but there's nobody to touch these people. . . I've seen men die in this war who would have won the Victoria Cross in another context.'

What was perhaps Williams's finest hour occurred in August 1968 when he led a 1,000-strong battalion of the Fourth Commando Brigade against an enemy column greatly superior in both numbers and equipment. Whereas his

Biafrans had only old-fashioned bolt-action rifles and a few mortars, the enemy had automatics, mortars, bazookas, machine-guns and armoured cars. What the Biafrans had, though, was enormous courage, backed by the inspiration of Williams and the skill of a Rhodesian mercenary called Johnny Erasmus. He was a dab hand with explosives and had learnt from the Biafrans how to make a home-made explosive device called an *ogbunigwe*. This was a contraption which, powered by dynamite, and fixed to the base of a tree trunk, would propel forward in a wide arc a lethal hail of ball bearings, stones, nails and the like. During the first day, Erasmus detonated at least forty of these devices, which cut swathes through the enemy infantry and even disabled one of their armoured cars. Erasmus' skill was even more important the following day, for by this time they had almost run out of rounds for their rifles, but still the Nigerians failed to break through, and the Biafrans maintained their position for nearly a week, and were forced to withdraw only because the town of Aba to their rear was taken in an out-flanking movement.

If Williams thrived in the difficult military situation, Steiner did not. The mental instability to which he had been prone in the past came to the fore, and finally led Ojukwu to dismiss him. Two days later, on 12 November, Williams led a Biafran attack on Onitsha, but in vain. Among the dead was a Flemish mercenary, Marc Goosens, whose death was dramatically captured on film—a stark reminder to the watching world and would-be mercenaries that the wages of war can be sudden, engulfing death. The following day saw another desperate attack, but again it was beaten back by the Nigerians. This was, indeed, about the end of the road for Williams and the few other mercenaries. They served out their contracts, but by early 1969 they were gone and not replaced.

Just as mercenary activity on the ground was drawing to a close, however, it was taking on a new lease of life in the air. At the beginning of the war a few foreign pilots, including one who rejoiced in the invented name of Kamikaze Brown, had worked wonders with the few wretched craft which comprised the Biafran air force, but after a while it had been completely destroyed, and control of the air had been left very firmly in the hands of the Nigerians. All this was changed, however, by a most unlikely character, a somewhat elderly Swedish pilot called Count Carl Gustav von Rosen. He was inspired to take the side of the Biafrans after he witnessed the grisly aftermath of a Nigerian air attack launched on the town of Umuahiah on Christmas Day 1968. He started off with just five small civilian aircraft—Minicons—which he transported to Biafra, then assembled and equipped with bombs and rockets. Then, on 22 May 1969, he, two other Swedes, and two Biafrans whom he had trained flew their first operation—a low-level attack on the airport at Port Harcourt. This took the whole world by surprise, and destroyed at least three Nigerian planes where they stood on

*Dr Jonas Savimbi's UNITA forces continue the battle against the MPLA long after the furore over Callan and his mercenaries has died down. Savimbi makes use of both Portuguese and other mercenaries to train and lead his troops* **(opposite page)** *while the MPLA still rely on Cuban support. Pictured* **above** *is a Cuban captured by UNITA forces at Lobito* (Camera Press, GAMMA/Spooner).

the ground. It was not, moreover, a mere flash in the pan. Further attacks followed, at first always against enemy airfields in order to try and destroy the numerical advantage that the Nigerian air force had, but later even against the oilfields which were so crucial to the Nigerian economy and so to the financing of the war. In the end, van Rosen's efforts did nothing to change the outcome of the war—victory for Nigeria and the collapse of the Republic of Biafra—but they certainly provided a valuable shot in the arm for the sagging morale of the Biafrans.

Biafra did not, however, blot out out the memory of Hoare's success in the Congo, and when the ill-fated British mercenaries flew out to Angola early in 1976, tempted by good money for an apparently cushy job insofar as they thought about it seriously at all, they seem to have believed that it would only take a few experienced British Army veterans to sort out the MPLA. In the event, their expectations were not entirely false. In the short time that they were out there, they did remarkably well in military terms, but the campaign relapsed into tragedy for reasons that had nothing to do with the calibre of their opponents. First of all, of course, a number of them were emphatically not battle-hardened veterans; these expected, naively, to be engaged only in training, transport and medical duties. Secondly Callan, for all his experience as a Paratrooper, and for all his unquestioned bravery under fire, was no Mike Hoare when it came to leadership. Indeed, of the mercenaries who went out, neither 'Colonel' Callan, nor 'Major' Hall, nor 'Captain' Christodoulou nor any of the others had ever officered troops before. While this did not prevent them gaining some considerable local successes, the campaign collapsed once Callan was injured and went missing. He left behind him no esprit de corps, and no command structure which would survive his loss, for what bound most of his men to him was fear—of his unpredictable behaviour and of the hostile environment in which they found themselves—rather than the admiration and respect which leads to deep-seated loyalty.

Colin Evans is interesting in this respect (see Chapter 6). He brands Callan, Christodoulou and Copeland as out-and-out killers, as psychopaths, and asserts that Callan deserved to die, but Evans followed Callan resolutely into battle and, when he was injured, carried him through the bush rather than abandon him to the enemy. In the end he left him to be captured only when Callan insisted that he do so with a wave of his pistol. When the chips were down, the army-bred qualities of loyalty and obedience to one's commander showed through, but once Callan was lost to the cause there was no individual, no body of officers, no sense of brotherhood to hold the cause together.

It would be a mistake to assume from the Congo, Biafra and Angola that mercenary activity thrives primarily in Africa. For although it continues to offer employment for professional soldiers, it is rivalled, and perhaps surpassed in this respect, by the oil-rich Middle East.

The mercenary boom began in the late 1960s, when the British began to withdraw their troops from the Arabian Gulf, and the wealthy rulers of the states in the region set about using their oil money to buy the soldiers and weaponry which they saw as essential to the security of their countries—and, it must be said, of their own, often repressive, regimes. In the ten years from 1966, for example, sales of arms to the Gulf states rose from £150 million to over £550 million—and the main beneficiaries of this financial bonanza were Britain and other Western countries. In addition, there was a vast amount spent on the hiring of military personnel; not only were these involved in the training of local troops, but they also took an active part in wars and in crushing revolutionary groups.

There had been mercenary activity even in the early 1960s in the region, but this had been comparatively small-scale. When the death of the Imam of Yemen gave rise to a bitter civil war there, a number of mercenaries who had been active in the Congo offered their services to the royalist forces of El Badr, but they never numbered more than a few dozen at any one time.

Those involved included the former French Foreign Légionnaire Robert Faulques, Bob Denard, Laboudique and the Flemish mercenary Goosens who would later die such a dramatic death in Biafra. There were even plans mooted, but never realized, to bring the whole of 5 Commando to the Yemen. However, the part played by these men was a far cry from the spearhead role which 5 Commando had enjoyed in the Congo. They were predominantly involved in training, and took comparatively little part in the actual fighting, as may be judged from the fact that only one of them—Tony de Saint Paul—is known to have been killed out there. Nor did they play a crucial part in the course of the war, and when Saudi financial aid to the royalists ceased, they quickly disappeared back to Africa, and to the new focus of mercenary activity there—Biafra.

Also active in the Yemen at the same time were some ex-SAS men, including a Major John Cooper and Colonel David Smiley, both of whom had previously served in the forces of the Sultan of Oman. The recruitment of these men seems to have been carried out with the unofficial encouragement of members of the British government, and according to Smiley the motive of these men were not purely venal—'not so much for the money as for the adventure'—and in the belief that their actions were in the interests

*Bob Denard, one of a number of mercenaries who fought in the Yemen (Camera Press).*

of Britain. A trio of them were killed in a particularly nasty incident. They put down their weapons at an enemy road-block thinking it that it was in fact a friendly, Royalist one, and were immediately shot down in cold blood and their bodies blown up with grenades.

Much more influential in historical terms than these wanderers were the many men who, from the late 1960s, were hired in increasing numbers by states such as Kuwait, the United Arab Emirates, Qatar, Bahrain and, above all, Oman. The majority of these were British. Britain may have been compelled to withdraw her troops from Aden, but she had no intention of letting her influence in the Gulf area decline more than was absolutely necessary. Oil, of course, was at the centre of Middle Eastern policy. Because oil was such a valuable commodity—especially in the pre-North Sea boom days—British governments considered it vital to preserve the existence of those local rulers who looked favourably upon them. If those rulers also happened to run autocratic, repressive regimes, then that mattered little as long as the interests of the West were safeguarded.

Oman was, and is, the prime example. In 1969 the Dhofar War broke out, when the autocratic regime of the Sultan was threatened by Communist-backed rebels. The British, to whom the Sultan appealed for help, were anxious to assist in every possible way a pro-British ruler in this key area of the world (the Sultan himself had been through Sandhurst), but they were equally anxious not be seen doing so. The result was a low-profile recruitment campaign conducted within the British Army to find men who would be prepared to serve the Sultan. There was no shortage of volunteers (including Ian, a Sergeant in the Parachute Regiment—see pp163-4) for work which offered plenty of action and extremely good rates of pay. At the same time, there was no loss of job security, for the usual procedure was for these men to be taken on 'loan service' which meant that after a two or three year spell they could return to their regiments in the British Army as if they had never been away, and having lost no rights or privileges in the meantime. This arrangement, as well as serving British interests in a covert manner, was also very rewarding financially for the British Army, for the Sultan paid not only the wages of the loan soldier, but also roughly as much again direct to the Army to make up, as it were, for the fact that these loan troops had been trained at the considerable expense of the British taxpayer. For the British, then, it was a doubly satisfactory arrangement. From the Sultan's point of view, it was for obvious reasons preferable if he could persuade his loan troops to sever all links with their home regiments and take out direct contracts with him. This was what a number of them did, and the Dhofar War was thus for them the start of a professional mercenary career.

The Dhofar War was a very drawn-out and hard-fought war, but ultimately it was won by the Sultan thanks to the help he received from foreign troops who provided leadership, training and specialist skills. Even when peace was

by and large restored, the Sultan continued to employ foreign troops and back-up personnel on loan service and contract to bolster his regime against his external, and internal, enemies. Men like Jim (see pp 164-5), who have earned in Oman much larger amounts of money than they could possibly have got elsewhere, and who have done so with relatively little risk to their own lives, have been instrumental in ensuring the continuance of the Sultan's regime. Indeed, these sort of men, in both Oman and the other Gulf states, have perhaps had a greater influence on the development (or lack of it) of world events than the more flamboyant wanderers who tend to hit the headlines. Much of their work may be involved in training local troops, and the governments which employ them will always stress that that is the case. But it first of all has to be commented that if you are a hired soldier involved in teaching others how to counter terrorist incursions, then you can hardly duck out of the way when the opportunity comes to put the training into practice. Secondly, training is not an entirely non-controversial thing to be doing; it does not just involve teaching men to use their equipment effectively, but also the maintenance of discipline and loyalty to the ruling employer, however enlightened or unenlightened he might be. Equally, the forces of Oman and other Gulf states are headed by foreign, usually British, officers. It may therefore be stated that the status quo of these states has depended and continues to depend to a significant degree on hired professional soldiers.

Not that the Middle East offers opportunities only for those mercenaries interested in long-term, comparatively non-dangerous contracts. One mercenary I spoke to had just returned from the Middle East following an assignment which lasted only a few weeks. He was loathe to reveal precise details of what he had been doing there, but he described it as being an 'anti-terrorist' operation which involved a period of planning, preparing and waiting, followed by a short, sharp piece of action near the Straits of Hormuz. He said that his next contract would take him to South Africa, which, he said, 'is where the action is going to be'. Several of his colleagues were already out there. What would he be doing there, I asked. 'You can guess the sort of thing.' 'You mean doing things which the South African military would prefer not to do themselves?' 'I don't need to spell it out, do I?'

All round the world, wherever war is being waged, and wherever regimes are under attack from 'rebels', 'guerrillas', or 'freedom fighters', there too mercenaries are likely to be found—in Africa, the Middle East, Central and Southern America, even in Sri Lanka. That island is wracked by a conflict between the numerically superior, ruling Sinhalese, and the Tamils, who would like to break away and establish themselves as a separate entity. The scenario which has unfolded there is typical enough: a minority 'rebel' grouping resorting gradually to more and more violent tactics and a government responding with increasingly vigorous military action. In such a situation, where military expertise is at a premium, governments are always liable to hire professionals to help themselves out of a difficulty. And that is precisely what the Sri Lankan president, Junius Jayawardene, did. He hired, through a company based in the Channel Islands and calling itself Keeni Meeni Services, the men with the skills that the situation required. These included ex-SAS and other professional soldiers, and ex-RAF and other pilots (one, at least, was South African) who respectively led government soldiers and flew helicopter gunships in ground and air attacks on Tamil positions. These men were reportedly earning a very credible £2,500 a month. Despite the fact that it was an open secret that these men were involved in active operations, the Sri Lankan government and Keeni Meeni Services both claimed that the mercenaries (not that they would ever use the word 'mercenary') were involved in training exercises only. Inevitably, too, the British High Commissioner in Sri Lanka insisted that 'we wish to make it clear that we have nothing to do with these people', and he admitted that if any of them were to be killed or captured (much more embarrassing, of course—dead men don't talk), then 'there could be grave diplomatic implications'. It was a statement which warned the mercenaries what they should already have been aware of already, that if they got into a fix, they would be publicly disowned. It is, nevertheless, hard to believe that unofficially and privately the activities of Keeni Meeni Services were disapproved of by the British authorities, especially after the Tamils bombed a civilian airliner, killing a number of passengers including three members of a Lincolnshire family.

Certainly, the two men who ran Keeni Meeni Services had the right sort of background to keep the right sort of contacts. David Walker was an ex-SAS major, and his colleague, James Johnson, had been an officer in the Guards. Prior to the Sri Lanka venture, they had picked up a very lucrative contract in the service of (who else?) the Sultan of Oman, which was reported to be worth in excess of a cool £12 million per year. Given the close relationship of the Sultan with the British Government, the deal could hardly have been obtained without the Foreign Office giving a tacit stamp of approval to KMS.

More interestingly, and even as this book was being written, KMS pulled some of their troops out of Sri Lanka and dispatched a small team to Honduras to train and fly missions for the Contras against the Sandinista government of Nicaragua. The leader of this small group was a former RAF pilot, Michael Borlace. He had spent three years from 1975 to 1978 serving Ian Smith's regime in Rhodesia, where he had been involved in flying helicopter missions against guerillas, and after that he was signed up by Major Ronald Reid-Dalby to serve in the tough irregular Selous Scout Force. He was driven by the usual motives — Reid-Dalby was reported as saying that Borlace wanted 'interesting and exciting' work and that he 'abhorred the idea of a humdrum existence'. He got his wish — and was sent as a member of an undercover team to Lusaka with the task of assassinating Joshua Nkomo, the leader of the Zipra guerillas. He was arrested, beaten up and tortured, spent over a year in gaol, and was finally released after Ian Smith's Rhodesia government had collapsed, being flown out to London following pressure from the Foreign Office. After that, he had to put up with less exciting but presumably more lucrative work flying helicopters for Arabs, before going out to Sri Lanka with KMS.

The KMS operation in support of the Contras does not seem to have been a success. Friction developed between the mercenaries and the Americans who were running the operation. The former accused the latter of having a 'Bay of Pigs mentality', and seem to have decided that the high level of risk involved in the way they were compelled to operate was not worth the money they were being paid, and within a few months Borlace and the others left Honduras to return to Europe and look around for another mission to satisfy their desire for excitement and money.

If mercenaries are often hired on long and short term contracts by governments to assist them against the threats posed by 'rebels' or 'freedom fighters', they are also on occasion hired to overthrow established regimes.

*The irony of the American attack on Libya in April 1986 is that it would probably never have happened if a mercenary attempt to initiate a coup against Gaddafi years earlier had not been stopped — by the Americans! This picture shows the damage inflicted on Benina airfield (MARS).*

BENINA AIRFIELD
15 APR 86

DESTROYED MIG-23/FLOGGER

MIG-23/FLOGGER PIECES

**Left** A US 'adviser' provides training in El Salvador (GAMMA/Spooner).

**This page** *There are few appropriate jobs for men who leave such groups as the Parachute Regiment, and it is no wonder that many of them end up doing what their training has best suited them for — serving as mercenaries. These pictures show Paras receiving that vital training (MARS).*

**Below left** *In America the same applies to ex-Marines, one of whom is seen here on regular service in Vietnam (US Marine Corps via MARS).*

The French Foreign Legion — the most famous mercenary body in history. The crisis of 1962 led to many ex-Legionnaires coming on to the mercenary market (Sipa/Rex).

Two members of the French Foreign Legion, dressed for the field rather than the parade ground (Sipa/Rex).

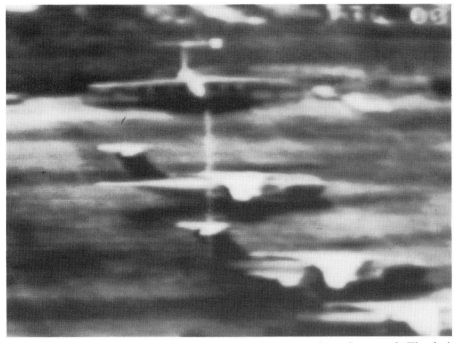

Photographs taken by a US plane as it attacks Libyan aircraft on the ground. The dark blobs in lower picture are 500 lb bombs (US Department of Defense via MARS).

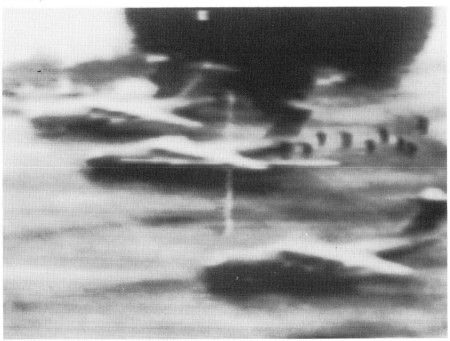

*President Gaddafi — target of the abortive 1970 mercenary operation* (Associated Press).

If Mike Hoare's abortive operation against the incumbent Seychelles government is the best known example of modern times, it is not, in terms of world history, a particularly significant one. Even if it had succeeded, it would not have had much effect on the course of events outside the islands themselves.

In April 1986, American bombers based in Britain flew across the Mediterranean Sea to deliver a bombing attack upon various sites and installations in Libya. The purpose of this dramatic attack, which had the personal imprimatur of President Reagan, was to try and put a stop to the terrorism which emanated from the regime of President Gaddafi. The attack was a heavy-handed attempt, born of frustration, to try and teach Gaddafi an old, gun-boat style lesson as it were, and Reagan may have hoped that it would also encourage Gaddafi's enemies to rise up and overthrow him. If so, his hopes were not fulfilled, and indeed the killing of civilians, including children, had the contrary effect. What was not remembered at the time, however, was the fact that none of this need ever have happened had a mercenary operation first planned in 1970 been allowed to be carried out.

Gaddafi came to power on 1 September 1969 when he led a coup against the emir of Libya, Muhammed Idris el-Senussi. Libya was a country whose wealth had increased by dramatic leaps and bounds during the 1960s— thanks to the discovery and exploitation of enormous oil reserves within her boundaries. The emir had been strongly pro-British and pro-West, and had allowed American and British military bases to be established within his country, but that all changed with the rise to power of Gaddafi. The radical new leader of this now important state quickly showed where his sympathies lay when he closed down the American and British bases, and he also expelled, along with Idris, many other pro-West Libyans who had accumulated great wealth from the 'black gold'. Many of these exiles fled to Rome, and before long a group was plotting a counter-coup which would, they hoped, topple Gaddafi and so enable them to return to their homeland and the source of their wealth.

What they required was military expertise—and if they did not have that themselves, they certainly had the cash with which to buy it. Before long, they took a crucial step in obtaining it when they made contact with a maverick South African who called himself Steve Reynolds. Not that Reynolds was a mercenary himself, but he could recognize an opportunity to make some money when it presented itself. He promptly went to London and there made contact with Watchguard, an organization based in the smart Knightsbridge area of London which specialized in providing military services—at a price, of course. Watchguard had been set up by Colonel David Stirling—the man who guaranteed himself a place in the military history books when in the Second World War he founded the SAS—and it usually provided military training and expertise to established governments. Being a 'respectable' outfit, it also took care to check out through contacts that any proposed mission had the unofficial blessing of the British authorities. To assist a group of exiles to overthrow an existing government would therefore be a departure from their normal mode of operation. Nevertheless, Stirling and his colleague James Kent took the proposal very seriously indeed. They had in the past had dealings with the deposed emir, and they were confident that the overthrow of Gaddafi would be in the interests of Britain.

From a military point of view, the proposed mission was eminently feasible. It merely involved attacking the main prison in Tripoli—jokingly known by the locals as the 'Hilton'—and releasing the many political prisoners held there. The released prisoners would then join other Libyans in carrying out the actual coup while the mercenaries could slip unobtrusively away from the scene and out of the country.

From a political point of view, it was not such a clear cut matter, however. It was one thing for the British government to want to see Gaddafi overthrown, but it was quite another thing for it to be thought to be involved, in any way, in a mercenary-led coup which achieved that result. Nor was Stirling happy that his Watchguard organization should be involved in such a venture lest it damage its credibility. He and Kent therefore agreed on a compromise; Watchguard would not be involved, but Kent himself as a freelance individual would, and he would, unofficially, be at liberty to make use of Watchguard's facilities and contacts. Stirling would maintain an interest and offer advice, but would not take any part in the detailed planning and carrying out of the operation.

They decided to spring the counter-coup by the middle of September 1970. The main military problem centred on the question of how to get into and out of Libya. In case the coup should fail, any mercenary who took part in the job would want to be sure that a reliable means of getting out of the country had been arranged. After some deliberation, they decided that the sea offered the likeliest opportunities. The mercenaries would sail to Libya from Malta and land under the cover of darkness at a sandy beach near Tripoli. Only some 25 men would be required—the overpowering of the prison guards was not likely to be a difficult matter for veteran soldiers—the whole mission should only take a couple of weeks, and the pay would be a tempting $5,000 per man.

At first, things went deceptively well. Twenty-five suitable men were found, vetted, and put on stand-by. Reconnaissance of the prison environs in Tripoli was successfully undertaken, and a suitable beach for landing from small craft was also found on the nearby coastline. In Malta, a number of small hotels were inspected, and bookings were made at several of them. Here the assembling mercenaries would stay for the two or three nights before their departure to Libya, and to Malta they would return when the job was done.

It was at this point, with preparations already well advanced, that Stirling was approached by both the British security services and the Foreign Office, and from both sources he received the same advice. It was, on reflection, considered that the use of British mercenaries in such a venture would—if their existence ever became public knowledge (which was, of course a very distinct possibility)—be a severe embarrassment, and therefore contrary to British interests. Britain would be accused by Arab countries of fostering the mission, and the political ramifications would be considerable.

Such firm advice was more than enough for Stirling. A patriot like him was not a man to go ahead with a mission which had received such an emphatic, unofficial thumbs-down. He therefore called off the operation, and had the mercenaries who had been hired paid off. But Kent, although he concurred in this, was not prepared to give up the whole idea. If he could not carry out the coup with British soldiers, then he would just have to use foreigners. Over the weeks which followed, he had several meetings in different places in Europe with Umar al-Shalhi, the former emir's closest adviser and the leader of the Libyan exiles. Shalhi, impressed by Kent's determination, fuelled it further by promising him a total fee of $4 million if the coup should be carried out successfully. As he said, such a sum was as nothing compared to the value of the oil which came out of wells in Libya every day. Again a mercenary team was put together, but this time it consisted largely of ex-French Foreign Legion veterans, the leader of whom was a former member of the 1er REP, who had survived the horrors of Dien Bien Phu and participated in the revolt in Algeria. He called himself Leon.

For a second time the mission was aborted, though on this occasion it was not the result of political pressure. The boat which had been hired to transport the mercenary team to Libya failed to arrive at Bari, and the shipment of arms which it was due to pick up en route was impounded by the Yugoslav authorities at Dubrovnik. Kent and Shalhi were furious, but they were nevertheless determined to try again.

Kent was now put in total command of the organization and execution of the operation. He promptly set about trying to ensure against any recurrence of the boat problem by buying one, the *Conquistador III*, and hiring a crew to sail it which he believed he could rely on. (As it turned out, he had trouble with the captain and had to replace him a bit later.) He also sorted out the problem with the arms, and had them transported to the pick-up point, the small port of Ploce on the Yugoslav coast, midway between Split and Dubrovnik. While the *Conquistador* was refitted at Toulon, Kent finalized the plans for this third attempt. These involved the boat sailing down the west coast of Italy, across the Adriatic to Ploce to collect the arms and ammunition, and then south to Catania in Sicily, where she would take on board the assembled mercenaries. As had been the case when Stirling and Kent first considered the mission, the mercenaries' task was merely to liberate and arm the political prisoners held in the 'Hilton' prison in Tripoli. They would then disappear back to the landing beach and to the refuge of the *Conquistador* while Umar al-Shalhi, the prisoners, and other supporters in Tripoli actually carried out the coup.

But despite all Kent's efforts, it was not a case of third time lucky. *Conquistador III* only made it as far as Trieste before the Italian *carabinieri* swooped, arrested all the men on board, and impounded the boat. They did so after receiving orders from a top-level meeting in Rome, but the decision to stop the coup was not, it seems, a purely Italian one. According to the journalists Patrick Searle and Maureen McConville, who wrote the full story of this whole remarkable business (*The Hilton Assignment*), both the Italians and, earlier, the British were pressured by the Americans to take the action they did. Searle and McConville argue that the Americans did so because, although they strongly disliked Gaddafi's anti-western and anti-Israeli stance, they nevertheless saw him as being extremely useful for his vehement anti-Marxism. If that is the case, then it is supremely ironical that in 1986 Reagan should order his airforce commanders to take the extreme step of bombing targets in Libya in a desperate attempt to bring to heel a man who, but for American interference, would have been overthrown long before.

The whole affair underlines the part which mercenaries may or may not be allowed to play within international affairs. The fact is that it is extremely difficult, if not impossible, for a mercenary operation of any size to be

*The US Army was glad to use mercenaries, like this long-haired Montagnard. Banks relates in his autobiography that he served in Vietnam for a year, often operating behind enemy lines* (Associated Press).

organized without its existence becoming known to the secret services of the country in which the mercenaries are recruited. It therefore follows that mercenary operations of this sort only go ahead if the host country tacitly approves the objectives of the mission. In short, mercenaries can be a useful tool to governments and secret services; they can be covertly assisted as necessary, but conveniently and ostentatiously disowned if anything goes wrong. (See Chapter 7 for elaboration of this fact of international politics.)

Across the Atlantic from Europe things are—in the field of the mercenary as in much else—decidedly and distinctively different. Indeed, the situation in the United States of America is a remarkable paradox. On the one hand, the USA is a country in which, in theory, mercenarism is illegal. On the other hand, American society is almost obsessed with the mercenary life, and the 'merc' is now big business. Not that this should come as any real surprise in a country where the word 'Communist' is like a red flag to a Rambo, and which can spawn a hugely successful TV series like *The A-Team* which peddles the dangerous myth that golden-hearted mercenaries can put the world to rights with a maximum of violence but no actual killing.

If the 'A-Team' is a fictional band of American mercs, though, there are plenty of the real thing operating in Central America and elsewhere around the globe. Nicaragua is one of the most recent centres of such activity. The left-wing, democratically-elected Sandinista government is for many Americans a major public enemy, despite the fact that it presides over a small and impoverished country. Because it is left-wing though, and because Nicaragua is situated in the USA's 'back yard', it has become the prime target of the many anti-Communists in Reaganite America. With the collusion and covert assistance of the CIA, American mercenaries are giving regular military support to the right-wing Contras who operate against the Sandinista regime from bases just across the border in Honduras. Under the terms of the Neutrality Act this is illegal, and anyone who operates as a mercenary from the United States is liable to prosecution. However, there is no political will to invoke the law, and US mercenaries continue to practise their way of life with impunity (see Chapter 7).

Further to the south, the much less publicized civil war in Surinam also attracts the attention of mercenaries from both the United States and Europe. The European connection derives from the fact that Surinam was once a Dutch colony. Some 200,000 Surinamese now live in the Netherlands, and the wealthiest of them use their own money to hire mercenary teams to go and 'liberate' their homeland. By its position, Surinam naturally attracts Americans. In 1983 an American mercenary who calls himself Dr John organized and led a coup attempt against the left-wing government of Colonel Désiré 'Desi' Bouterse, but it was not successful. However, the centre of resistance now comes from a former member of Bouterse's bodyguard, Sergeant (now Captain) Ronny Brunswijk, who enjoyed some dramatic successes during 1986 thanks in no small measure, it would seem, to the presence of foreign mercenaries amongst his guerrilla/rebel forces.

The man who may reasonably be described as the doyen of American mercenaries is Robert K. Brown. A veteran who has fought and trained troops around the world, his most distinctive achievement has been in the field of publishing rather than war, for it was he who established what may be termed the first widely-read mercenary magazine. *Soldier of Fortune* is grandly sub-titled 'The Journal of Professional Adventurers', and was established to cater for the needs of American mercenaries and would-be mercenaries. Thus it includes reports on the areas of conflict in the world where opportunities exist for mercenaries; it provides analyses of the latest military weaponry and equipment; and it contains an extraordinary advertisement section. The magazine's success has been so great that it has inspired other publishers to cash in on the same market. Thus *New Breed* calls itself 'The Magazine for the Bold Adventurer', and *Gung-Ho* ambitiously describes itself as 'The Magazine for the International Military Man'.

The vast majority of the people who read these publications are not, and probably never will be, mercenaries. For them the idea of being a 'merc' is pure (or should I say 'impure') fantasy, and although they may never become 'guns for hire', they can at least read about those who are. But some of the readers of these magazines—in particular *Soldier of Fortune*—are active mercenaries, and for them such reading material helps not only to keep them

*Soldier of Fortune* and other similar magazines enjoy great popularity in the USA and are marketed around the world.

'Soldiers of fortune' at a get-together in the USA. They dislike the terms 'mercenary' and 'merc', seeing themselves as patriots furthering their country's interests abroad (GAMMA/Spooner).

*Until 1986,* Soldier of Fortune *contained many advertisements placed by active or would-be mercenaries.*

abreast of relevant events around the world, but also perhaps to obtain work.

To read through the several pages of advertisements which appear in each issue of *Soldier of Fortune* is an eye-opening experience. There you can find such dubious publications as the *Minimanual of the Urban Guerrilla* which covers, the reader is promised, 'firing teams, ambush, sabotage and bank assaults'. There are a whole host of weapons, from the latest combat knives to a 'Laserstun' gun which 'shoots high intensity rays that blind'; alternatively you can buy a booklet which shows with diagrams how you can make your own machine-gun; or you can purchase the latest electronic surveillance equipment; or, indeed, you can be your own mercenary.

A typical advertisement is:

'FOR HIRE: ex-Paratrooper, team leader (long-range patrol), Rangers (instructor), three tours Vietnam, scuba, seeks employment in related field. Will train-lead-organize. Preference given to Central America.'

Those who advertise often take pains to stress that they are serious, experienced professionals:

'SOLDIER FOR HIRE: Expert small arms, rifles, demolitions. Prefer South Africa, all others considered. No James Bond or Super Spook. Just good soldier.'

Or:

'CONTRACT MERCENARY AVAILABLE: Just completed five years in the Middle East, eager for another contract, short or long. Two years experience in Africa, one year in Central America. Ex-US Special Forces member with expertise in weapons, demolitions, recon, rescue, patrol, scuba, parachuting, training and insurgency tactics. If you are looking for a proven professional please contact me. All work is considered but please do not waste my time if you are not looking for a true professional. Assignments must be on contract and completion basis.'

In some cases you can even hire small teams at a stroke, as with the following advertisement (shades of the 'A-Team'!):

'EX-VIETNAM TEAM SEEKS EMPLOYMENT outside US or anything legal inside US. Expertise in long-range recon, rescue, explosives and engineering, light weapons infantry.'

It is not clear how effective such personal advertising is. One man told me that he had a number of people ring him and write to him in response to his advert, but 'about seventy per cent of them were nutters'. However, he admitted that he did make a few useful contacts and felt that the expenditure of a few dollars had been well worthwhile. (It is not just 'nutters', though, nor genuine employers of mercenaries who scan the personal adverts. A couple of cases have been brought to court in which men convicted of bank robberies were alleged to have been hired after their advertisements appeared in *Soldier of Fortune*, and, even as this book was being completed, this has caused the editors of that magazine to ban such personal adverts.)

But if you are a would-be mercenary, and feel you are not quite up to it, you can always go to school:

'PARA-COMMANDO SURVIVAL SCHOOL! Southern California area. Learn survival skills in natural and man-made hostile environments with comprehensive weapons training.'

There is a lot of choice and competition:

'MERC. BEFORE YOU GO FOR THE BIG BUCKS, GET THE PROPER TRAINING. Some of the other mercenary schools claim to be the originals which makes them the best. NOT SO! They advertise realistic combat training but actually use *non-firing* replica firearms and tear gas spray.

*The forests of Little Rock Canyon, Alabama, provide a fine setting for one mercenary school. For a sizeable fee, would-be 'mercs' learn how to handle different types of weapons, how to live on their wits, and how to stalk and hide from their foes (Rex Features).*

**Above** One potential mercenary learns the hard way that a gun is not always enough against a stealthy enemy (Rex Features).

**Right** Mercenary schools like to keep things totally realistic. The guns are real, and the instructors often use live ammunition to keep their pupils' heads down (Sipa/Rex).

**Below** A female mercenary gets to grips with weapon handling (Rex Features).

*Frank Camper shows how to assemble an M-16. He prides himself on the toughness and realism of his school for mercenaries.* (The Photo Source).

THAT'S REALISTIC TRAINING? Send $1 for our brochure.'

Some of these schools cater primarily for the individual who wants to test himself to the limit for reasons of personal satisfaction, but others openly claim to be in the business of training would-be mercenaries. Certainly the courses they lay on are extremely arduous, and are taken by men with military and, often, mercenary experience. Frank Camper, a Vietnam veteran who has fought freelance in the Yemen, El Salvador, Guatemala and Mexico, prides himself on the fact that his school makes no concessions. Unarmed combat training involves hitting—and being hit by—a fellow student with no holds barred. Fighting with heavy, padded pugil sticks is a standard part of army training, but at Frank Camper's school the only protective equipment allowed to the participants is a helmet, whereas in the US Army recruits are always heavily padded to prevent injury. In the escape and evasion part of the course, enormous pressure is kept on—the trainers lay innumerable booby traps, use live bullets, attempt to take individuals prisoner in ambushes and then blindfold and knock them about as if it was for real. Furthermore, students never know what is going to happen next, so that the maximum mental pressure is exerted on them. 'If you tell people beforehand what the limitation of anything is, they can pace themselves. But

*Whatever the advertisements may say, mercenaries do not always earn huge sums of money. These French 'volunteers' claimed to be fighting for the Phalangists in Beirut essentially for the cause — food, and a packet of cigarettes a day, was the total of their 'pay' (Rex Features).*

going into something open-ended is stressful.' If you get injured, there is no quick trip to the local hospital. As Camper put it, 'On real merc operations, there is usually no way to get anybody out for treatment. I try and encourage a hurt student to stay in the field. We dress the wounds out here. If it's really necessary—life-threatening—then of course we get the man out.'

A course at Frank Camper's school is no easy ride. The whole business is taken very seriously. Many of the students are foreigners, who have been sent by their home countries for further military training. And others, unquestionably, are men who want to be, and will be, mercenaries. Everyone who survives the course and is judged to have passed automatically becomes a member of the Mercenary Assocation which, while it cannot legally act as a mercenary recruitment agency, does the next best thing by providing its members with all the general and detailed information which they are going to need to find themselves 'foreign employment'.

Strictly speaking, mercenary schools should be illegal in the United States for the Neutrality Act makes it unlawful to operate as a mercenary from within the country's borders, but there are loopholes which make it difficult to enforce, as well as a distinct lack of will to do so (see pp 207-12). One day, perhaps, they will be clamped down on. But it may not be for some considerable time yet. In the meantime, they encapsulate the American obsession with the merc way of life, and provide those who are serious about hiring themselves out as professional soldiers with a chance to sharpen themselves for the experience.

'Vive la mort! Vive la guerre! Vive le sacre mercenaire!' is the toast of all those who make the grade at Frank Camper's school. It is an emotional, romantic refrain. But it should not be allowed to hide reality, which is often harsh, dirty and anything but romantic. The experience of one man who advertised himself in *Soldier of Fortune* may be taken as a powerful antidote. Daniel Gearhart requested 'employment as mercenary on full-time or job contract', and professed to be ready to go 'anywhere in the world if transportation is paid'. But the confident wording belied a desperate man. To try and make the 'big bucks', he paid his own way out to Angola, was captured, tried (his advertisement was used as evidence against him), and shot by a firing squad.

The romantic image of the highly paid roving merc is also undermined by the experiences of another American mercenary, David McGrady. His mercenary career began in Rhodesia as a bodyguard for the Rhodesian Ministry of Health. Three months later he was bored by the lack of action, and so he headed to Matabeleland where he found more interesting work protecting ranchers and bounty hunting. He proved good enough at the latter to have a price put on his own head by the terrorists, and so he moved on again. He then signed a contract with the Somoza government in Nicaragua just before it fell, and when he returned to Africa, his hopes of successful bounty-hunting in the south-west went for a burton when drought ensured that the ranchers would have no need of his protection. So he went back to the United States, and after hanging round for a while at last he got his chance of a 'real' war—fighting for the Christian Lebanese Forces of Free Lebanon for the princely monthly wage 480 Lebanese livres, less than £100 a month or, as he put it, 'just enough to cover the cost of cigarettes and beer until the next payday'. Not quite the big bucks he must have hoped for. Vive le sacre mercenaire!

## Chapter 5

# What makes a mercenary?

'A spirit of adventure, an ex-soldier's difficulty in adjusting to civilian life, unemployment, domestic troubles, ideals, fanaticism, greed—all may play some part in the same individual's motivation.' Report of the Diplock Commission.

There is no single, simple answer to the question which this chapter poses for the simple reason that the term 'mercenary' encompasses such a wide variety of types of people. And these people are motivated by a similarly wide variety of different things—a desire for money, a sense of adventure, a need to prove something, idealism, a love of soldiering and, last but not least, sheer desperation. What follows, then, does not even pretend to be a definitive answer. Rather it attempts to show, through a series of cameos, the sort of men that mercenaries are and the types of thing that make them tick.

Despite the impossibility of making precise definitions, it is convenient and useful to attempt to categorize, as far as is possible, the different types of mercenary. 'Mark', a British mercenary active today, provides a starting point when he divides mercenaries into two camps: those who deliberately chose to leave the army, and those who were dishonourably discharged. Since Mark places himself in the first category, his judgement might be thought to be somewhat prejudiced, but what he says has a strong element of truth. When asked to explain further, he said that when he speaks of people being dishonourably discharged he is thinking in particular of a number of those who went out to Angola. That is to say, men like Callan, Wainhouse and Hall, all of whom were kicked out of the Army after they were convicted of criminal offences. There were, however, plenty of Angola recruits who had not been dishonourably discharged, just as there were even some who had never served in the Army. Nevertheless, Mark's categorization is an interesting and useful one, not least because it reflects his feeling that it is such people who bring what he feels is an honourable trade into disrepute.

Another way of categorizing mercenaries might be as 'professionals' and 'amateurs'. The former would be those who do it more or less full time for a living, the latter those who perhaps only do it once. The latter might include men who fight for one particular cause because they feel strongly

**Left** *What makes a mercenary? The motives are multifarious and the reality of the life is equally varied. For a Frenchman fighting in death-ridden Lebanon, the pay is virtually non-existent but the exhilaration presumably makes up for it* (Rex Features).

**Below** *But a Portuguese, Manuel de Assuncio, fights with the FNLA in Angola because he came to the country at the age of 10 and never left* (GAMMA/Spooner).

**Above** *It is for the training of troops that mercenaries are often required, both in terms of weapons practice . . .* (Camera Press).

**Right** *. . .and to put their pupils through the toughening up procedure which will prepare them for battle* (Camera Press).

about it, but most especially those who take up a mercenary assignment because it comes up by chance when they are feeling desperate. That was certainly the case of many of those hired to fight in Angola. But again, this categorization cannot be pressed too far.

## A British legionary

One man who was very much a professional mercenary is Geoff Richardson, formerly of the French Foreign Legion. A measure of the man can be gauged by his card to me when he replied to an advertisement which I placed in a national newspaper, asking to meet anyone who hd been engaged in mercenary work.

'If by "mercenary" you refer to armed thugs, in army surplus clothing, killing native people without other thought than high pay and getting "kicks", then I do not qualify.

'If you mean honourable volunteer service, in a foreign land under a foreign flag for little pay, but much hope of glory and adventure, you may contact me.'

His story begins like something out of a novel. He ran away to sea at fifteen, and for three years worked on merchant ships. At eighteen, after he was laid off in London, he returned home briefly, and had a row with his father who thought he was wasting his life. 'He said something like: "You'll come home

when you're hungry"; and that spurred me on. "The hell I will", I said. And just like that, overnight, I bought a ticket across to France, and went up to the first policeman I saw, as if I was fulfilling my destiny, and told him that I wanted to join the French Foreign Legion.'

In Paris, a recruiting officer and a conscript did their best to dissuade him from taking the plunge. 'You realize you're in for five years? Your consul can't help you during that time. The only way out is mutilation or death.' But these warnings were ineffective, and after being given a night to think it over, he signed up the following day.

In Richardson's case, motivation that came largely from within—a sense of adventure, an independence of spirit, a need to prove something to himself and to a critical father. It was in the mid-1930s that he joined the Legion, and he was soon to see a considerable influx of new recruits from amongst those men who had been serving in the International Brigades in Spain against Franco. Many of these, driven back to the frontier, had been given the choice of joining the Legion or being handed over to the Spanish authorities. Not surprisingly, they had opted for the Legion, but despite the circumstances of their recruitment, Richardson found the 'the idealist motive was very strong in them'. This was also true of many of the Germans in the Legion who, at the outbreak of the Second World War, opted to fight against their homeland because of their hatred of the Nazi regime. They did so

**Left** *Obote and Okello review their troops — but the hiring of foreign troops to assist in 'training' could not keep them in power* (Camera Press).

**Right** *Ultimately, all mercenaries run the risk of capture, and whatever that might lead to — a show trial, imprisonment, or a bullet in the back of the head* (GAMMA/ Spooner).

knowing that they could expect no mercy if they were captured.

In due course, Richardson and a number of his comrades in the 11th Regiment were captured after mounting a rearguard action in a forest near Verdun in June 1940. The most senior of the prisoners was Richardson's company adjutant, a German, and in the hope of avoiding detection he pretended to be a Frenchman. His impersonation was not, however, successful, and when his true nationality was discovered he was taken behind the nearest building and shot. A more traumatic experience still awaited Richardson, however. He escaped to Paris, but after a couple of months he was recaptured together with a fellow légionnaire called Bauernfeind. They were both taken to Memmingen, and there they were interrogated by the Abwehr. While Richardson was made to wait in an anteroom, his friend Bauernfeind was subjected to intensive questioning in an adjoining room, the connecting door being deliberately left ajar. The Germans had researched Bauerfeind's background and had discovered that he was from the Sudetenland. They now proceeded to interrogate him in the hope of getting him to confess. When he stubbornly refused to admit it, the Abwehr officer picked up a heavy, ebonite desk rule and 'proceeded to beat him round his head until he died'. Richardson, listening next door, is haunted to this day by the final defiant words of his friend: 'Ich bin keine Deutsch. Ich bin Czechische!'

After the war, Richardson was honourably discharged by the Legion and was awarded the Croix de Guerre. He returned to Britain and married a midwife, and settled down in a 'steady' job. His 'mercenary' career was over, though in the 1960s he was very much tempted to go to the Congo and serve under Mike Hoare. He was encouraged to do so by the fact that an old friend and comrade, a Brazilian called Albert (he was head barman at the Café de la Paix bar at the Place de l'Opéra in Paris) had decided to go to the Congo along with a couple of other ex-légionnaires whom he knew. 'I knew they were not just cut-throats—they were real men—so I was all set to go.' But in the end he changed his mind, first because he was very put off by a couple of men whom he was told to contact in Camberley—'there was a lot of booze being sloshed about, and I couldn't believe that this was going to be an efficient deal'—and secondly because when he went to Paris to finalize matters—his work took him there regularly—he found that Albert was no longer working in the Café de la Paix but had been taken to a clinic where he was receiving treatment for cancer of the bowel. With Albert now unable to go (he died shortly afterwards) and having been put off by the men in Camberley, Richardson decided not to go after all. What had attracted him most about the venture was the opportunity to recreate the camaraderie which he had enjoyed in the Legion, but this was something which was singularly lacking at Camberley where 'booze and cash' were the main topics of conversation.

## Thoroughly modern pros

If Richardson is, by the criteria of this book, almost ancient history, 'Mark' is very much a mercenary of the present day. He left the Army of his own volition, because the active service and excitement which he had hoped to find in the Army could be found only in Northern Ireland. Now he is a professional mercenary. He lives with his wife and two children in an isolated farmhouse in the north of England, where he indulges in his favourite pastimes of gardening and fishing—a far cry from the popular caricature of hard-bitten, hard-drinking loner with a kink in his character. He finds no difficulty in obtaining work, and is in the position of being able to pick and choose. Most contracts take him to Africa or the Middle East.

An illuminating slant on his profession is provided by his wife. She lives a life of two sharply divided parts. When her husband is away she makes sure she has plenty to distract her. Apart from two children to look after, she holds down a job and socializes a great deal. When he returns home, she cuts right down on her outside activities and her friends know to stop asking her out. It seems a hard life, not least in the winter when snow invariably cuts the farmhouse off from the rest of the world for days at a time—indeed, in the winter of 1984/5 it was nearly three weeks before a farmer on a JCB dug a track through to her. But despite all this, she nevertheless finds it in some ways a less stressful life than when Mark was serving in the British Army. Above all, she used to hate it when he was doing spells in Northern Ireland. 'Every time you watched the news, Northern Ireland used to be on—a bombing or a shooting—and you couldn't help thinking about him and wondering if he was all right. It was impossible not to worry about him.' By contrast, she finds it easier to come to terms with his being absent now. Although she obviously thinks about him, there are no regular news bulletins, no daily paper to constantly underline the danger in which he may be.

Mercenary contracts are not necessarily fraught with danger, especially if you are careful about what you take on and what you don't. Furthermore, they are lucrative, and whereas Army life used to involve uprooting the family and moving house every two to three years, she now has a fine house which acts as a secure base. Even so, uncertainty is something that goes with the way of life, as I discovered at first hand one September morning. Mark was due to arrive at my house with a colleague for a meeting, but half an hour before he was due to arrive the phone rang.

'Mr Tickler?'

'Yes?'

'This is Mrs ---. I'm afraid my husband can't meet you today as he's gone abroad. He received a phone call late last night asking him to catch an aeroplane. I've only just got back from driving him there.'

'Oh!'

'I would have rung from Heathrow, but I didn't have your number on me. I'm afraid this is one of the hazards of the job. He doesn't know when he'll be back. Maybe a week. Maybe a month. But he'll be in touch then.'

If Mark can be called away at the shortest notice, the timing of his return can be equally uncertain and unsettling. His wife rarely knows how long a job is going to last or when precisely she can expect to see him again. Indeed she has learnt the hard way that it is best not to expect him until he walks through the door. The very first time he was away on a freelance contract, she received a phone call after a few weeks saying that he would be back the following Wednesday. Not surprisingly, Wednesday couldn't come soon enough for her, but finally it arrived. However, as the hours passed, and morning turned to afternoon, and afternoon to evening, there was no sign of Mark, and no message to say that he was safely back in the country. Thursday came and went, as did much of Friday, until the phone finally rang. Hardly daring to do so, she picked up the receiver and heard his voice telling her that he had just landed.

Those 48 hours were some of the most fraught of her whole life. 'I was worried sick. I was convinced that something must have happened to him. I couldn't imagine that he wouldn't have been able to phone me and warn me that he would be later than planned. I was convinced that he was dead.'

They have learnt from the experience. Now, when a phone call comes, she is told merely that he'll be home in the following week. Nothing more specific. And she tries to forget about it and continue her life and that of her children until the phone rings again and she hears the words: 'I've landed.'

If being a freelance mercenary is for Mark a deliberately chosen option, for another British mercenary, John, it is much more a means to an end. Formerly in the British Army, he denies that he is in the mercenary trade because soldiering is the only thing he knows. It is, he admits, the thing he can do best, but he is also involved in the licensing trade, and his goal is to set up and manage his own bar. That will involve capital outlay, and so that he can realize his dream he trades on the job which the British Army taught him to do. He averages two or three contracts a year, and they are of comparatively short duration, a matter of weeks rather than months. Yet the pay is good—he reckons never to receive less than £5,000 for an assignment.

When questioned about the nature of what he does, about the risks which he faces and the fact that it may well involve killing others, he is remarkably matter of fact. 'To me, it's just a normal job. . . You could be working in a factory and get caught in a lathe or machine. It's just about the same risk to me. . . It's the job I know I can do best.' He admits that he has had to kill people while on mercenary assignments, but does not know how many. 'You don't keep a score of the numbers. It's just part of the job.'

When pressed about the morality of killing, he displays the standard argument of the soldier. That is what the job sometimes involves. Personal conscience is irrelevant. In so far as he rationalizes what he does, he argues that if he and his comrades did not do it, then someone else would, and 'they might go around butchering everybody'. It is much better, he implies, that there should be people like him around, thoroughly professional in their approach, who will kill only where 'necessary', and otherwise not indulge in excessive bloodshed. It is an amoral line of argument, honest to a point, and not lacking in its own cold logic. Whatever one feels about it, it is hard to deny that in the modern world, as in the past, the men who wish to employ mercenaries will always be able to find ex-soldiers who will take their money and do their bidding.

In stark contrast is another modern mercenary, the American mercenary and recruiter Dr John. Where John is straightforward, Dr John is dramatic. Where John speaks of mercenarism being just a job, Dr John speaks of anti-Communist ideals and personal satisfaction. Dr John insists that his 'original impetus is altruistic'. 'I believe in what I am doing. I'm a private citizen actually impacting world events. There's a lot of reinforcement, a lot of gratification there.' But he would not do it if he was not paid well. 'I have to make a living at it of course, or I couldn't do it for very long, or I'd be crazy to do it.' He also admits to getting a real kick out of dangerous military work. As he rather overdramatically puts it, 'There's exhilaration from knowing that every step on the jungle path might be your last. It's not duplicated in civilian life.'

Dr John is no mere trained gun for hire, though. As well as being an active participant in covert operations, he also recruits for and organizes them. Thus in 1983 he led an attempted coup against the government of Surinam in South America. His expertise is not just in the handling of guns and other weapons. 'What I in particular have to sell are my connections, my contacts, in the world of munitions and arms, and in international transport and international banking.' This makes him extremely marketable. He can command a fee of anything between $2,000 and $5,000 per month plus expenses, and even at that price he claims to never be short of offers of work.

Also very active is 'Don', who served a dozen years in the Royal Marines, and has since done a variety of things including working on North Sea oil rigs. But it is covert military jobs at which he now makes a living. When I asked him why he did it, he refused to put it down simply to money. The money, he admitted, was good—'very lucrative in short spells'—but that was only part of it. When I suggested that he was attracted by the excitement, he metaphorically shied away from the word. Mercenary work, he insisted, was certainly not pure excitement. Much of the time was spent 'sitting and waiting', and the action, when it came, was all over in a matter of minutes. He did, however, confess to having 'itchy feet'. He had no desire to settle in one job in one place. And mercenary work certainly serves to satisfy the lust for new places and new situations. His work is what he usually describes as 'anti-terrorist', and has taken him to many different places—the Middle East (inevitably), some European countries, different parts of Africa—and when I spoke to him he had just accepted a job in South Africa, which is 'where the action is just now' he told me. Work comes to him by and large through the personal contacts which he has built up over the years, though he did once publicize himself in a personal advert. Of those people who replied to it 'seventy per cent were nutters', but he did neverthless receive some genuine calls which led on to work.

## The gun or the hod?

Another man who has been heavily involved in the recruitment of mercenaries is yet another John—John Banks. He hit the headlines in 1976 as a result of the leading part which he played in the recruitment of mercenaries for the war in Angola. He has been much maligned for that, but however fair or unfair such condemnation may be, it is more important to understand how he and many others came to be mercenaries. It certainly was nothing to do with a desire to 'impact world events'.

His first step on the road to being a mercenary may be said to have been taken on 2 September 1962 when he signed on with the Parachute Regiment. The name of this unit keeps recurring throughout these pages. Callan and

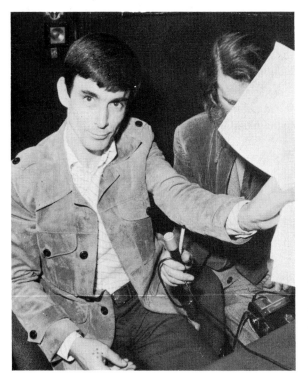

*John Banks, a classic example of the ex-Para who could not settle to civilian life, and who preferred the excitement of mercenary service to the tedium of a building site* (The Photo Source).

the three men with whom he first flew out to Angola were ex-Paras. When Banks himself was looking for men to fight against the MPLA, it was to his former Para mates that he first turned. When the British Army was covertly looking for men to fight in the gruelling Dhofar campaign, it was from the Parachute Regiment that it found its keenest recruits.

The reason why so many British mercenaries are ex-Paras may be put down to the fact that they are 'bloody good soldiers'—the Parachute Regiment does, after all, pride itself on being the best. But that begs the question: what is a 'bloody good soldier'? What is it that marks out Paras as being the best, different from the common run of British soldiery?

The Duke of Wellington once commented of a particular unit of his army in the Peninsular War: 'I don't know what they do to the enemy, but by God they frighten me!' It is a remark of uncomfortable insight, and one which strikes at the very heart of the whole question of attitudes towards mercenaries—indeed at the heart of militarism generally. For the truth of the matter is that the 'bloody good soldier' is often not a bloody good civilian. As Banks wrote in his autobiography, he was trained in the Parachute regiment to 'be aggressive and to kill without compassion'. A man trained to be a ruthlessly efficient killer is hardly going to be the nicest person in the world. If he was he just wouldn't have made the grade.

Those people who do thrive in the environment of the Parachute Regiment are precisely the sort of people who find it difficult to settle down to 'ordinary' life once they have left the army. One ex-Para told me that he deliberately chose not to marry and raise a family, despite being tempted to do so, because, 'It seldom works. Most of the regiment are cowboys.'

It was an expression which I couldn't help recalling when I read the early part of John Bank's autobiography. It is easy to condemn his role in the Angola fiasco, yet he was a man who had proudly passed out as the best recruit of his intake after an exhaustive Para training. Banks' account of himself, even allowing for some exaggeration and embroidery, reveals a not untypical Para figure: a man of great bravery and resources, who thrived on the hazardous and difficult situation, a man unable to settle down, a womanizer, no respecter of ranks or persons, quick to use his fists to settle an argument and unwilling to settle for a humdrum existence.

Most instructive is his account of his transition from the Army to life outside. He was discharged from the Parachute Regiment on 10 June 1969, following a conviction for driving a car without insurance and while disqualified. He skates over this reason for his discharge in his autobiography, preferring instead to stress the growing disillusionment he felt over the changing role of the British Army and the decreasing opportunities for the action and excitement on which he thrived. 'Some of us would never settle down to peacetime soldiering; we felt as if we were redundant.' As well as Banks, some seventy other Paras were to leave the regiment in the next six months, and whatever their reasons for leaving they all came up against the same problem—what to do in civy street.

Banks records how he went down to the local labour exchange to see what work he could get. The young man on the other side of the counter asked what he was qualified to do, but Banks' explanation that he knew how to parachute, handle a variety of guns, and kill people caused hardly a raised eyebrow. There were plenty of ex-Paras in Aldershot. 'Well, Mr Banks. We can offer you the same as we offer most other ex-Paras that come in here—labouring on a building site.' Neither the reply, nor the disinterested manner in which it was given, were to Banks' liking. 'I felt like breaking his neck. Here I was, a professional soldier from the proudest regiment in the British Army, a man who had been proud to serve his Queen regardless of risk, and the little bastard couldn't be bothered to spare me more than a couple of his precious minutes.' Banks' words encapsulate the almost insuperable problem which faces Paras when they transfer from the Army—where they are encouraged to believe they are the very best—to civilian life where they are valued very lowly indeed, good only for the building site. Banks had tried that before he joined the army, but his propensity for getting into brawls meant that he was never at the same site for long. So he joined the Paras where, as he comments, he at least got paid for fighting.

All this goes to underline the truth of what a padre of the Parachute Regiment said to Sergeant Ian and some of his comrades after a particularly hard day of dealing with their personal problems. 'It's all very well. You Paras may be able to face death, but you can't cope with life.'

The case of Callan is instructive too, for accounts of his behaviour in Angola make it clear that, whatever his shortcomings, there was no doubting his personal bravery. Indeed, he seems to have had that quality to the point of recklessness—and beyond. In the same way, perhaps, he had the qualities of single-mindedness and ruthlessness—neither of which the successful soldier can afford to be without—to an excessive degree. It is easy to condemn his execution of his fellow mercenaries in Angola, but he was certainly not the first man to kill a fellow soldier in the field on the grounds of cowardice.

All of the original 'gang of four' who were the first British mercenaries to be hired by Holden Roberto to fight in Angola—Callan, Hall, Wainhouse and Christdoulou—were ex-Paras, and all four had, like Banks, had to face the problem of what to do when they left the Army. Initially they had drifted into the inevitable building work, but that did not satisfy their lust for action and the hope of making big money. They did not like life outside the Army. They could face death, but not the humdrum life of a civvy. It is no wonder, then, that they drifted into the Angola business. If that had not come up, doubtless something else would have, which required them to use their Army-trained skills.

For men like these, motivation is not some nebulous desire for adventure.

rituals to decide retribution'

**Desperate 'free my son' plea**

Callan says 'my orders followed'

**MERCY PLEA FOR THE DOGS OF WAR**

**Wife's plea to husband in Angola**

Yorkshire soldier jailed for 24 year

# Callaghan acts as mercenaries face execution

**PROBE OVER 'HELL JAIL' ORDEAL**

*Mercenaries are news, and the Angola episode produced an endless stream of stories and headlines from every possible angle.*

It is something which service in a regiment as tough and ruthless as the Paras has nurtured and encouraged in them. Resourcefulness, immense powers of endurance, an ability to kill efficiently without second thought—these are the things for which they were valued when they were in the Army. Once out, they discovered that such qualities made them unsuitable temperamentally for many jobs, and suitable only for jobs involving covert military action or lucrative but less fulfilling bodyguard work. It is no wonder that they became mercenaries. For many, it must be the case that signing on for the Paras is, if they make the grade, the first step towards a mercenary career.

## A US trio

The Angolan war attracted very few Americans, but the thirteen mercenaries captured and later tried by the regime of President Neto included a trio of 'mercs' from the USA. Gustavo Grillo, Daniel Gearhart, and Gary Acker had all served in Vietnam, but apart from that their backgrounds and careers were distinctly different.

Grillo was Argentinian by birth, but had emigrated to the USA with his mother at the age of eleven. In 1966, aged seventeen, he had joined the US Marines and, after a shortened training period, had served in Vietnam from 1967 to 1970. He had had a 'good' war, rising to the rank of platoon Sergeant, 'always at the front. . .patrols by day, ambushes at night'. But like his British counterpart, he had found the transition from soldier to civilian difficult. In his written testimony to the Angolan court, he described how he returned home to the States in 1970 'with letters of recommendation, but with no training for normal civilian life. I managed with great difficulty to get a job as a mechanic, etc. I began to work in construction, but I didn't make enough money to live.'

Ill-equipped for life outside the Marines, both practically and, after a highly stressed time in the front line, psychologically, Grillo now drifted almost inevitably into one of the few lines of business for which his military skills

*Gustavo Grillo had a 'good war' in Vietnam, but could not adapt to civilian life after coming out of the US Army. He drifted into crime and, finally, mercenary activity (GAMMA/Spooner).*

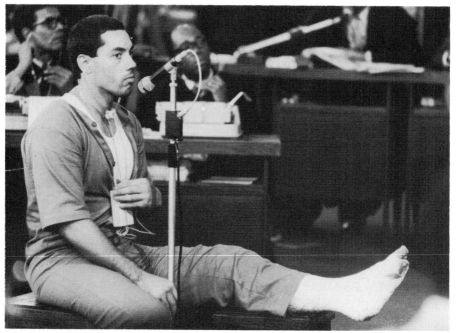

suited him—crime. 'I began to get involved with gangsters I knew, for more money—always some dirty business.' Involvement in this 'dirty business' led ultimately to his arrest and conviction for armed robbery. When he had served his eighteen-month sentence, however, he found getting legitimate work even harder than before, and soon drifted back into crime, as a bodyguard and debt-collector for a crime boss.

Gary Acker had also served in the US Marines, but his Vietnam experience was confined to the aircraft carrier USS *Ranger*. He acted as the guard of its stock of nuclear weapons, while the ship patrolled the seas off the Indo-China coast—a mobile base from which American bombers plastered the Vietnamese mainland. Acker returned to the USA after a year and a half, but had problems coping with the demands of Service life. He failed to get into the US Naval Academy, later went absent with leave for four months, was consequently demoted from the rank of Corporal to Lance-Corporal, and was referred to a psychiatrist. He underwent group therapy, but was later diagnosed a 'severe schizophrenic passive aggressive' and, in 1975, was demobilized. However sound of mind he had been when he first entered the Marines, there is no doubt that he left a psychological wreck.

Acker and Grillo did not consider the possibility of becoming mercenaries until they learnt through the media that David Bufkin was looking to recruit men to fight in Angola for high rates of pay. The third member of the wretched trio, however, Daniel Gearhart, was already actively looking for work in the latter part of 1975. Driven by the pressures of debt, he advertised his services in the magazine *Soldier of Fortune*. 'Wanted. South or Central America, but anywhere in the world if you pay transportation.'

At much the same time, Dave Bufkin was attempting to establish himself as a mercenary recruiter—via small adverts in newspapers, and through interviews in *Soldier of Fortune* magazine and on television. He even flew out to Angola where he met Holden Roberto, but although he then returned to the USA to hire recruits, he had very limited success because of lack of money. The CIA was anxious that American citizens should not become involved as mercenaries in Angola, and for that reason Bufkin—unlike Banks in England—was unable to get hold of the cash which he needed to turn his dreams of a mercenary army into reality. Not only was he unable to offer advances, but he could not even afford to pay the air fares of the men who contacted him. Since American mercenaries would also risk losing their citizenship if they got involved in a war in Africa, it is no wonder that there were very few who were willing to accompany Bufkin across the Atlantic, and they were a wretched selection driven by desperation above all else.

Furthermore, once out in Angola, they quickly discovered that Bufkin had painted a picture which bore little relation to reality. Acker claimed 'My entire association with Bufkin was one of deceit on his part'. When he had met Bufkin at Fresno, California, Bufkin had told him that there were 'vast numbers of mercenary troops in Angola'. Once out in Kinshasa, however, Acker and the others swapped experiences and quickly concluded that Bufkin was a liar, whose primary motive in recruiting them had been to make money for himself. As a consequence, they held a gunpoint court martial, found Bufkin guilty, fined him $200, and reduced him to the rank of ordinary soldier. Bufkin had been intending to return to the USA where he claimed to have a hundred recruits ready and waiting to fly out to Angola, but his jury insisted that he stay in Angola and fight.

In the event, he managed to commandeer a light aircraft and fly himself to freedom, whereas Gearhart, Grillo and Acker remained to face the music. The latter two were sentenced to long spells in prison by the Angolan court, and Gearhart was condemned to death and executed. His demeanour in court was his ultimate undoing. He foolishly claimed not to be a mercenary as such, but to have come to Angola because he was interested in politics. When the judge commented that it was 'a little strange that someone who wants to study the political situation comes as a mercenary', Gearhart replied 'It's the only way I could come. I came to study people.' But this was a ridiculous assertion to make, especially as the court had the hard evidence of Gearhart's advert in *Soldier of Fortune* asking for 'Employment as a mercenary', and they were also able to reveal that he was a member of the Wild Geese Club, a club for mercenaries established in South Africa. Indeed, Gearhart's unrepentant attitude in court and his ineffectual attempts to deny he was a mercenary were counterproductive, and he, along with Callan, Barker, and McKenzie, was shot on the orders of the court despite the protests of foreign heads of state. By contrast, Grillo, who admitted that he had come as a mercenary, and who also attacked the USA, CIA and FBI in court, ensured by such means that he was given only a prison sentence.

Daniel Gearhart advertised his services in Soldier of Fortune, *a fact which was greatly to his disadvantage when he was tried in Angola as a mercenary. His claim that he 'came to study the people' failed to save him from execution* (GAMMA/ Spooner).

# The Oman connection

Since the 1960s, Oman has been a haven of mercenary activity. Because of its position in the oil-rich Arabian Gulf, and because of the strong connections of the Sultan with Britain, the British have since that time actively assisted the Sultan in the maintenance of his regime. Initially, this was in the long drawn-out and hard struggle against Communist insurgents known as the Dhofar War, when many soldiers were 'loaned' to his army. These soldiers often later severed all contact with the British Army and took up private contracts with the Sultan. But even since the successful conclusion of that war, the Sultan has continued to employ many foreign soldiers, most of them British, to uphold his pro-British, but autocratic regime.

Typical is the story of Ian, a Sergeant in the crack Parachute Regiment. In 1969 he was completing his first term of twelve years in the regiment, and was wondering whether to sign on for a further ten years, which would qualify him for a pension. 'Part of me wanted to do the usual things, marry and have children and have a house, etc. However, I was really aware that I would not settle down for long, and as the worst thing to be is a married Para, I thought I would do the extra time.' Before he signed on, however, he was summoned by his Brigadier who offered him the alternative of serving in Oman. The idea appealed to him, and after an interview in London, he was offered and signed a three-year contract to serve as a Captain in the army of the Sultan of Oman. The promotion from Sergeant to Captain was one of three reasons why he was happy to take the job. ('I must have gone snobby', he joked.) The other two were the traditional ones of 'the thought of adventure' and money. His pay was substantial, 'the equivalent of a British Colonel plus no tax, no mess bills, and no dreary Routine Duties'.

Since the recruitment of British Servicemen to fight for the Sultan of Oman was politically sensitive, Ian was left under no illusions about the importance of being discreet about the whole business. At the same time, the British government took every step it could to ensure that the Sultan's requirements were met. Thus once Ian had signed his contract, he was given special training, first at the Royal Military Academy, Sandhurst ('I had a great time. . .getting the feel of being an officer!') and then with the SAS, which he found 'very hard work both physically and mentally as the instructors never let up and rank counted for nothing'. Because he was 'on loan', Ian did not lose any of the benefits and rights which service in the British Army had entitled him to, and he was assured that he would remain on the sub-stantive roll of the Parachute Regiment during his three-year contract, which meant that if he wished he could return to the regiment afterwards. In fact, after his three-year spell he chose to go 'on contract' with the Sultan—he formally severed ties with the Paras and for the next five years owed his allegiance entirely to the Sultan, who not only continued to pay him very handsomely, but also took over his pension rights. When Ian did finally return to Britain from Oman, however, he was recommissioned into the Territorial Army as a Parachute Regiment officer 'at the discretion of the MOD', as he says.

His is a fairly typical career, though there were others for whom service in Oman was the stepping-off point for a continuing freelance career. In Ian's case, this was not an appealing prospect. One of the reasons why he enjoyed the Oman experience so much was because the military was run very much along British lines, and after eight years he was happy to return to the relative comfort of the Territorials.

His years in Oman had been anything but comfortable. He found the Dhofar War 'hard and pretty scary at times', and saw a number of his British colleagues die, as well as many more of the Arab troops under him. 'The worst problem was mines and the second one sickness. We patrolled mainly on foot at night because the enemy seemed to be able to see and hear us when we had no idea of their presence. During the day it was also too hot to move, so we ate and slept and kept radio watch. Water was a problem as we had to carry all our own supplies for eight to twelve days, so we had to rely on replenishing from streams if available or wells. The men could be very tricky at times—it always seemed impossible to understand an Arab's way of thinking; just when one thought one had clicked his reasoning, he would go and act in an opposite way. We had a number of desertions to the Ado, but also men who fought terrifically.'

Oman offers, and will continue to offer for some considerable time to come, good prospects for the British Serviceman seeking a change. Certainly 'Jim', who has served in Oman since 1979, is thoroughly satisfied with his experiences out there. When I asked him why and he so many others opted for the Middle East, and in particular for Oman, he told me that the expatriates put it down to the three Ds—Divorce, Debt, Despair. A joke maybe, but like every good joke not so far from the truth. For himself, he admits to considerable disillusionment with his career in Britain, where he had become desk-bound with nothing to look forward to except retirement. However, the main reason why he decided to uproot and go to Oman was the money.

Like so many others, Jim started work in Oman on loan service. After two years he took several months leave in Britain, then returned to Oman, this time as a contract officer. Initially he had to accept a drop in rank—he was later promoted—but since he was immediately earning significantly more than he been in Britain, this was of no real concern to him. A family man with plenty of financial worries, he went unaccompanied to Oman, but soon the scale of his earnings, plus those of his wife at home, transformed the situation. He readily paid off all his debts in Britain, and was thereafter able to save a substantial amount so that he longer actually needs to work in Oman. A Major (or equivalent in other armies) currently earns nearly £2,000 per month, and special allowances (such as for flying) are payable on top. Furthermore, this pay is worth considerably more than its equivalent in Britain because it is tax free. Even ignoring the no-tax bonus, Jim could not hope to earn nearly as much back in Britain as he does out in Oman, even if he could find a job that suited him. But it is not just the money that has induced him to keep on accepting extensions to his contract in the Sultan's forces.

The fact is that he gets a lot of job satisfaction. Firstly he is not desk-bound—which is what he had virtually become in the British forces—and secondly he is allowed plenty of initiative to do his work as he sees fit. While he is not allowed total licence in the way he operates, the restrictions are much less than in Britain, and he also finds that his expertise is fully respected. Oman is a particularly favourable environment for Brits in so far as there are many supervisory positions open to them, and they are still respected by the Omanis for what they are and can do. By contrast, Arabs hold sway in the majority of other Gulf states, and the general feeling amongst the expatriate community is that they are notoriously unwilling to discipline their fellow Arabs.

Although the Serviceman who applies for a post in the army, air force, or navy of Oman may be driven to do so through personal or financial problems, he has to go through a stringent vetting procedure before he is offered a contract. Oman is very far from being a bolt-hole for anyone trained to fire a gun or fly a plane. A high code of conduct is expected—transgressors soon find themselves out of a job—and Jim feels that the ethos is neither as rigid nor as stuffy as that he encountered in Britain. He feels he has always been treated very fairly, and sums up the treatment of himself and other ex-Servicemen as 'very loyal, very fair'. At the same time he is well aware that one mistake could see him on the next flight home—indeed, for this reason he was surprisingly nervous of talking to me even though he has few criticisms of his treatment and life in Oman. The main drawback from his point of view is that his family are unable to be with him, although they have visited him from time to time.

In every other respect, he finds life in Oman very agreeable, not least because it is so Western and European. In Oman, being British counts, and it is that fact above all else which makes the country such a pleasant financial oasis for the British Serviceman who hasn't got everything.

*Chapter 6*

# One man's nightmare

This chapter is the edited transcript of an interview which Colin Evans gave me. He was one of the nine mercenaries imprisoned by the Angolans after a show trial in 1976. He was given a 24-year sentence, but was released in 1984 along with his fellow mercenaries. No mercenary has ever been imprisoned for longer, and Evans has hitherto refused to talk publicly about his long ordeal.

It is a story of a man who drifted into mercenarism out of desperation; he served under the notorious Callan and remained loyal to him until Callan was on the point of capture; he endured a trial for his life; he started his prison sentence as an object of distrust and hatred, and ended it enjoying, remarkably, the confidence of the authorities; and, finally, he returned home, to a new life—and no job.

It is a sometimes harrowing, always human story. Evans himself is remarkably philosophical. 'I can't say I regret doing it, because I don't.' His bitterness is reserved, not for Callan (who he calls an 'out-and-out killer'), for the Angolans, or the Cubans (who treated him very well), but for the British—the government because it took so long to get him released, and the faceless authorities who have refused to renew his HGV licence, so that he can now get no worthwhile decently paid job.

*'What is your military background?'*
'It started on my seventeenth birthday when I signed on with the King's Own Yorkshire Light Infantry for a period of ten years. After a basic training, I was posted to my battalion, and a few months later—August 1965 I think—I flew out to Aden. We did ten months there, normal policing work, patrols and suchlike. I did two tours on the border and saw some action there against the Yemenis. After that we returned to Tidworth in England, and after a short spell there we went out to Berlin for two years. There were a lot of duties and guards—mostly pretty boring. In 1969 we returned to England, this time to the barracks in Colchester. I then had three months in Malaya, most of it in the jungle, and on my return to Colchester I got myself a nice posting—a nice cushy number—as barman in the officer's mess down in Bulford, Wiltshire. I did two years there, and when I returned to the battalion, I was asked what I would like to do. I said I would like to go into

the regimental police, but after about ten weeks in Northern Ireland, I felt a bit down with the Army, and so I applied for and got a transfer to the Royal Corps of Transport. I passed a basic B3 drivers' course with flying colours, and after that was posted to Munster, West Germany. I spent two years over there, and after that my ten years in the Army was more or less up.'

'*Why did you leave the Army?*'
  'I had had enough. I wanted to be a civilian again. I'd had enough uniforms and orders to last me a lifetime. And on top of that I was having personal troubles with my first wife which I don't want to go into.'

'*What did you do between leaving the Army and going to Angola?*'
  'Well, while I was in the RCT, I managed to get myself an HGV Class 2, so I went lorry driving. I was doing a lot of long-distance work until the time I left my wife in June 1975. I then returned to my home town of Dewsbury, where I got a job driving a small lorry delivering roof tiles. It was very, very low paid—I think I was bringing home about £30 a week, and on top of that I was getting pressured for my maintenance and I just could not manage. It was getting me down, and it got to a stage where I wasn't bothered and I'd have done anything.'

'*How did you first hear about Angola?*'
  'Well, I happened to be visiting my father's bungalow one day, and he showed me his paper—I think it was the *Daily Mirror*, I'm not sure—and it was on page two. It said they were looking for people to go out to Angola as training staff, medical orderlies, things like this you know—which was a load of rubbish. I felt I'd give it a try. I phoned up the newspaper, and they gave me a chappie's address down in Norfolk. I phoned him, and he took my name and in turn gave me a phone number. I can't remember where it was, now, but when I rang it I think it was John Banks I spoke to. He said he would phone me back later on in the week. This was the Monday, I think. Anyway, on Friday my father came looking for me. He said "I've had a phone call from this gentleman. Will you ring him back?" I did do, and this chappie said, "Would you be prepared to go out to Angola?" I said "Yes". He said, "Right. Can you be down at Victoria Station underneath the clock about twelve o'clock, where there'll be someone to meet you. There's many people going, and you'll get all your details there."'

'*So why exactly did you decide to go to Angola?*'
  'Well, I decided to go because of the money. Obviously, £150 in 1976 was a lot of money, and I was only earning £30 a week. On top of that, I wanted to get away from things and sort myself out. Really, I wanted to get a lot of money together, because I'd thought of buying my own lorry, starting my own business up, and seeing what I could do there. I couldn't pay for my kids,

I couldn't give them nothing. I had nothing in my pocket, and I thought this was a good way out of it.'

'*Had you ever thought of doing mercenary work before this?*'
'No, I hadn't. I had never even given it the slightest thought. It was the first time and as far as I am concerned now it was the last time.'

'*Did Banks tell you what you would be expected to do out in Angola?*'
'Yes, Banks did, along with his henchmen. In the hotel, we had a big meeting, and he outlined what was going on. He told us about Callan, and how good he was and what he was doing. And he also told us we would be training black Africans, Angolans, men of the FNLA. A lot of us didn't really believe this, but we let him carry on. It doesn't take much commonsense to know when a bloke's telling lies. We knew he was out on the make. We did hear he'd made a lot of money out of us—how much we'll never find out. We knew we'd end up fighting, but I suppose a lot of us accepted that.'

'*What about the trip out to Angola? What was that like?*'
'Well, it was a bit of a farce really. There were two flights. I was in the second one. We had breakfast in the hotel on the Wednesday, and then we were all given little badges to stick on our lapels. We were supposed to be some sort of diet people, going on a conference about various foods and that. It was a farce. Anyway, we got on the bus, and when we got to Heathrow, Banks got on the bus and he came to every single one of us and said: "I'm going to pay you now the first week's wages in advance. If anyone decides to get off the bus and do a runner, I'll look for them and they'll be for it." Anyway, Banks handed me an envelope with £150 in it. I took about £20 out, put the rest in a separate envelope with a stamp on it, addressed it to my sister in Yorkshire and once I got off the bus I posted it straight away.

'Some of us had not got passports—me for one. Mine had run out shortly after I had left the Army. We had already had passport photographs taken in a booth, and we were given these small cards to fill in by the immigration people. We filled them in and assembled in a big group. As I said we hadn't got passports, and the immigration man just made a phone call to someone— I don't know who—and five minutes later he waved all the lot of us through, no problem. He didn't even check the blokes' passports, cards or nothing. They knew what was going on. I think he must have got in contact with some intelligence folk. Anyway, we all got on the second flight—it was a charter flight—to Brussels. It was a nice flight. When we got there, we were all waiting in the arrival lounge when we happened to look out the windows and we saw armoured cars posted at various positions around the airfield. Inside the building there were quite a lot of armed police with sub-machine-guns. They kept a nice steady eye on us and they kept us all in a big group. Anyway, we took a Boeing 707 belonging to the Dutch company Sabena out of

*Banks leads a group of mercenaries, amongst them Colin Evans, on to a plane at Heathrow, destination Angola. After paying them earlier on the bus, he had warned them against 'doing a runner'. He had said he would come looking for anyone who did. (The Photo Source).*

Brussels, and the flight to Zaire must have taken us about nine hours. Unbeknown to us, a lot of cases had been loaded into the hold of the aircraft. We found out later that these contained anti-tank rockets—not the RPG7, but the American one, the disposable one.'

*'What happened when you first arrived in Kinshasa? Were you impressed by what you found?'*

'We arrived in the early hours in the morning; it was cold, very cold at that time of night, and we were hungry. We were taken across Kinshasa to Holden Roberto's palace, where we were met by some of the Angolan liaison staff. We were given a drink and all our equipment if you can call it that. It was all Belgian "seconds", I think, or "thirds"; the weapons were the Belgian FN, the M1 carbines, American stuff. We had to take a pair of boots out of a big pile, all odd numbers; if you were lucky you got a pair of socks. It was a farce, a complete farce. When we were kitted out, they decided to take us for a proper meal. They organized a coach, and we went into Kinshasa to the Hotel Intercontinental where we had a fairly decent meal and a bottle of nice cold beer.'

*'When you did meet up with Callan?'*

'During the night they took us from Kinshasa across the border into Angola. We ended up in a place called Sao Salvador, where we were met by Callan, and by Copeland. As soon as we got off the coach, he had us all fall in at the front and he gave us all a good dressing down. He said what a load of scruffs we looked. He said, "First thing, haircuts". We were all taken inside where we had our hair cut down to about a quarter of an inch. Anyway, we stopped there—the building was Holden Roberto's summer residence—had a meal, got ourselves sorted out, and finally Callan says 'Right, we're all moving. We're going to a place called Maquela. It's about four or five hours ride.'

'We set off south for Maquela. It's a bad road and it was raining. It wasn't an iron or asphalt road, it was a dirt track. We went through gullies where the rain had washed the dirt away, and we got bogged down many times. We travelled all night. It should have taken us about five hours, but in fact it took about ten. When we got to Maquela, we had a meal of rice, sardines and some black coffee. Then Callan got everybody outside and fell us all in in two

**Above and left** *The MPLA and their supporters were by and large well equipped, but the British and the other mercenaries supporting the FNLA were much less so. When they first arrived in Kinshasa, they were offered a motley collection of old weapons, but later picked up better equipment in the course of events in Angola (Camera Press).*

ranks. Then he went to each man individually, and asked him what he had been in. Now there had been some talk and a bit of unrest because of us moving south. When we were in Kinshasa, a lot of the lads hadn't wanted to go south, hadn't wanted to enter Angola. They thought they were on to a cushy number stopping in Zaire and training black soldiers. But they found out this was not so, that they were due to go fighting. Callan wanted to know what military experiences we had all had. A number of them hadn't any whatsoever. Some had never even been in a uniform or seen a rifle. They thought it was a big game, some of them. We had even got one or two Royal Navy chaps there. We had even got a bomb chappie who hadn't been in the army and he was an interpreter. He spoke fluent Russian. Callan didn't like this. Anyway, he separated us all out, put the chaps who hadn't any military experience on the one side and the chaps who wanted to fight, who wanted to stay, on the other. I think at the time Callan was in the mood to send these chaps back. He didn't want them; they were no good to him. They had no experience, they were a danger to the rest of us. We'd have to carry them, and show them what to do, and it's not easy in a combat zone. You have to know what you're doing.'

(Evans then told me how he was one of a party of troops who accompanied Callan on a journey some miles north to a village occupied by some Zairean troops. Callan hoped to borrow their tanks for an attack, but despite half an hour's discussion with the officer, he was unable to persuade him. Shortly afterwards, Evans again accompanied Callan on a trip, but they drove at such a speed that one of the Land Rovers turned over and injured one of the passengers. Evans then drove his vehicle to Sao Salvador to get an ambulance, and it was after seeing the injured man into the ambulance that he learnt that the enemy had, apparently, taken the village of Maquela.)

'We were on the way back to Maquela when we were stopped on the road by Callan and a few of the men. Apparently, from what we could make out, Maquela had come under attack. Now all the fighting men were out. The only people at Maquela were the lads who didn't want to fight. They'd been left on light barrack duties—as cleaners, cooks, you name it. Apparently, one of our vehicles had gone into Maquela, and these lads thought it was the MPLA, and they had opened fire on it. They'd used rifle fire, machine-gun fire, and also anti-tank rockets.

'So Callan stopped us all at a small village a couple of miles outside Maquela. We were going to mount an attack, and recover Maquela, at first light. It had been dark for a couple of hours, so we bedded down where we could. Next morning, we made a slow entrance into Maquela. We didn't see no enemy soldiers, no nothing. Callan wasn't very pleased at all. He saw our Land Rover, which had gone into the town, on its side, wrecked, and when he saw it he went mad. But the men who wouldn't fight had all gone. So we set off in pursuit of them.'

*'You caught them and brought them back. Can you tell me what happened then? Did you realize that Callan was going to have them shot?'*

'Callan decided to sort them out. He'd had enough. So he lined all the men up who had refused to fight, and he lined the rest of us up in two rows in front of them. We were armed, and they weren't. They had had their weapons taken off them. Callan had also got a few of his own cronies who had been out there some time all around us, including some Portuguese. They had got guns on us, and we couldn't do a sodding thing. Callan picked on one young lad. He said, "You're the one who fired the rocket" and the man said "Yes, Sir". Callan took his pistol out of his holster, a 9 mm, and he shot him three times in the head. We were all dumbfounded. We just could not believe that he had shot one of his own men. He told the rest of them to strip their clothes off. He'd had enough. But he said there was a chance for some of them, and he picked out six who were willing to fight. As for the rest of them, he told Sammy Copeland, "Get them on that jeep and take them down the road. You know what to do with them." They all scampered onto the back of the vehicle with two or three of Callan's cronies. Copeland was in charge. And off they went. We didn't really think they would do anything to them. Anyway, we went and had a meal inside the building, and then we heard machine-gun fire in the distance. As it happened, Callan was there, and he just smiled. I thought, "You rotten, lousy sod, what the hell have you done?" Anyway, shortly after this the vehicle returned, and Callan said, "Right, we're moving out, we're going to mount an attack". So we all piled in the vehicle, and down the road about three or four miles we came across a steep bank going down to the left, and as we were passing we could see the bodies of our countrymen lying there. Anyway, we carried on to the front line, but we were all in shock, we just couldn't believe what had been going on.'

*'I think that it was soon after this that your batch of mercenaries first engaged the enemy. Can you tell me what happened?'*

'We met up with the rest of Callan's men further south, and then we all set off in a convoy, I was driving one of the anti-tank guns, and on board I had a Portuguese gunner and two Angolans, and about thirty to forty rounds of ammunition. We'd also got more ammunition for the gun on a short-wheelbased Land Rover, literally stacked high with them. On the way south Callan ordered us to keep over to the side as we had reached a minefield, one of our own. But it looked to us as we went past as though the minefield had been moved. Shortly afterwards, a long-wheelbased Land Rover carrying small arms and men in front of me hit a mine. The vehicle itself went up into the air about thirty feet, and I also saw two men spreadeagled about thirty feet above the Land Rover, and they just sailed to the ground with a terrible thump. Automatically we all stopped and went to give assistance. There was blood everywhere. Three of the men were dead, and the others on the vehicle were dazed. Callan came back and ordered one of the rear vehicles to take the dead men along with a couple of the men who were injured back to Maquela.

'Little did we know, but the MPLA were only a few miles down the road, and the explosion gave them a chance to set up an ambush. And a big ambush it was. But fortunately for us, they opened fire on our little column about fifteen to twenty seconds too early. Normal British tactics are, when you run into an ambush, you stop, get out, and go straight in towards them. This we did, though I didn't personally. I stayed back with my gun. There was a lot of fire about. We replied with a big gun. But they had tanks, and there were also mortar shells coming over. We gave covering fire to where we thought the enemy was. We know for a fact that we did a lot of damage. We also saw tanks from their rear moving towards us, and we opened fire on them. Later on, after we had been captured, we found out that we had knocked out three tanks. The whole attack lasted about 45 minutes. Callan and his men had gone in and caused a lot of damage, and we later learnt that they suffered 163 dead and many, many wounded. When Callan returned, all our men were present, with one or two wounded. Only one was serious: a man had nearly lost his arm, which was literally hanging on; but he managed to make it back to England. We boarded the vehicles and went back to Quimboco. Callan was happy, he was in a joyous mood. When we reached the place where the Land Rover had hit the mine, there were a few tin shacks, and Callan, being in the good mood that he was, decided to machine-gun the shacks. Whether there was anyone in them, we didn't know. He reckoned that it was these people in the shacks who had moved the mines, which they were quite capable of doing. They were MPLA supporters.'

*'So what happened next?'*

'The very next day Callan decided that we'd hit the enemy again. So we split up into groups, and we were to be known as Killer Group One and Killer Group Two. I was in Callan's killer group of twelve men. I was also given a weapon called a widowmaker, that's a grenade launcher. I took as much ammunition for this as I could carry, and I also had a Chinese Star pistol with four magazines. Callan said we weren't to take any extra food or water as we would only be out for 24 hours, but we were to carry as much ammunition as we could.

'We drove for about ten miles, then stopped the vehicles, got out, and continued to advance in two columns through the bush on foot. We came to a village as it was getting dusk, and Callan decided we'd stop there till early dawn. We continued south at dawn, and after about an hour we crossed the road and climbed into some hills. Looking down from the hills, we could see a lot of movement a couple of miles further down the road. It was the enemy front line; they had got a bulldozer, and they were clearing the road of mines. There was also some armour, and a lot of soldiers, Cuban and Angolan. Later in the afternoon, Callan decided that we were going to go down there and see what we could do. So we proceeded south and round the back of the enemy front line. We walked along the side of the road; there was a mound, where the bulldozer had been, all along the side of the road. We were about two miles behind the front line, still heading south, when we heard some vehiles approaching. (Incidentally, the two groups had by this time joined into one). There were two vehicles: one was a Russian equivalent of our Land Rover, and the other was a four-door Renault. Callan shouted, "Snap ambush!"

'So as they passed, we opened fire with everything we had got. We literally made them look like colanders. Both vehicles crashed into the side of the road, and one man escaped from the Renault and started to run up the road the way he'd come. Callan ordered this man to be stopped. One of our chaps jumped out into the road and opened fire. He had a semi-automatic, and he must have fired a lot of rounds, but he missed. I got on to the road and fired two shells from my grenade launcher. I saw one shell go sailing over his head, the second one I don't know what happened. Suddenly, there were explosions all round us. The enemy had got our position, and they were dropping mortars on top of us. So we all bugged out. By this time it was getting dark, and we followed Callan into the bush. We knew from the past that the MPLA did not like going into the bush, especially at night. They are very superstitious, so we knew they wouldn't come after us.'

*'And what happened then?'*
'We now started heading north towards the MPLA front line. We passed an armoured vehicle right next to a wood, and we touched it. We all touched it. The lid was closed down, and they were snoring inside; they were all fast asleep. We continued for a couple of hundred yards, to their front line. Things had got quiet by this time. They were having their evening meal; there was the rattle of plates, a lot of laughing and joking. We got within a hundred yards of these people. There were no sentries. We could see what we thought was a tank, so we decided to hit it. We had brought with us about forty anti-tank missiles. With these, and my grenade launcher, and two or three other grenade launchers we had with us, we all opened up. All of a sudden there was such an explosion. We thought we had hit the tank and it had exploded. We had destroyed it, in fact. But the blast threw us all over the place. I went back about ten yards, and my weapon went up in the air along with many others. Then all of a sudden it just started raining fire. My clothes were on fire, and everything. Quickly I detached all the shells I had left—about thirty or forty—because as I say I was on fire and if they had gone up I think everyone around me would have perished. Callan had been

injured by the blast. He had been hit by shrapnel, as had one or two of the others, so we got out. The enemy had been hurt bad too—they were in the middle of the explosion—and we didn't think there'd be many survivors.

'That is the time that everything went wrong. We broke up completely. Ten or eleven of us grouped up together—Callan was one of them, Copeland another. We took shelter two or three hundred yards down a track from the ambush and stopped there until daylight. Next morning we started to proceed north-west, or was it north-east? Anyway, we were heading home. Callan was hurt, and he was hurt very bad. We'd got a medic with us, who had given him an injection and splinted his leg which was broken high up on his thigh. Callan knew we needed help, so he sent Copeland and a Portuguese off to get it. By this time there was Callan, myself and six others. We carried Callan on a makeshift stretcher, hoping to get him to a hospital, and after a while we came to a grove with a hut. There were people in the hut, and when they came out we waved to them. They waved back, and came and helped us carry Callan inside. It was the home of Isabella Senda and Antonio, her husband. We made Callan comfortable, the medic gave him another injection and changed his dressing, and then we had a meal. The very next day, Callan sent a couple of chaps out to a nearby village to get a doctor and some food. These chaps went, and shortly afterwards we heard a lot of machine-gun fire and we knew they had run into trouble. Copeland had not returned as we hoped with a helicopter, and after about four days we decided to move out from the home of Isabella and Antonio. This woman and her husband were treated quite well. I even showed them a photograph of my own children which I carry with me. They were given little trinkets, a cigarette box, and things like that, and they were not mistreated in any way whatsoever. People have said that they were mistreated. They were *not*.'

*'So how did you come to be captured?'*
'Well, we were down to just six of us, including Callan. We put him on a stretcher, with four of us carrying and one man leading the way. We hadn't gone far when we came across a patrol, about a hundred yards away. At the same time we saw them, they saw us. We got down in the tall grass, and Callan said "Leave me". We refused and said, "We're not leaving you. We don't do that. We're taking you with us." He just pulled a pistol out, turned round on us, and said, "If you don't, I'll shoot you myself. Go!" Four of us stuck together, but the medic went off on his own, and I didn't see him again until I was in prison.

'All that time we were maybe three weeks in the bush. We had no food, no map, no compass. We had two rifles, one of which didn't work. We had no water, no nothing. By the end of the second or third week, I was so weak. . .at one point we were ambushed and I lost my boots. . .I was very sick, in fact I honestly thought I was dying. I could walk a hundred yards, then I had to rest for ten minutes. Anyway, we came across a village and three of the lads decided to go into it and get some help. This was late in the afternoon, and by nightfall they hadn't returned. I could see the village across the river, which I wasn't capable of crossing. In the morning three Angolans came across the river looking for me. They came up to me, put some flip-flops on my feet, helped me up, and they also gave me a cigarette, my first one for about a fortnight—it was beautiful. Then they helped me along this little track to a place where they could ford it. They let me make my own pace, across the river and then up the other side towards the village. But about a hundred yards from the village I heard the sound of vehicles. At that very moment, the men who had been so kind to me grabbed me, forced my hands behind my back, and tied them there. They then started to run me along the stubble grass—I had no shoes or socks and they had pulled the flip-flops off me—my feet were bleeding and swollen, and they were hitting me in the back with a big knife, flat side on. The two trucks stopped in the village, and one of the men came running across when he saw us and hit me full in the face with his fist. Then an officer—I think he was Cuban—said something to him and the man backed away.

'Soon I saw the other three lads; they had been taken prisoner too, their hands were tied behind their backs with steel wire, and they looked in a terrible state. The officer put us on a truck and we set off to where we didn't know. About three or four miles outside the village we stopped, in a little grove. Naturally, we all thought "This is it. This is where we get a bullet in the head." But we were wrong. They started picking mangoes off the trees. Since we were tied together, the Angolan soldiers offered us mangoes, holding pieces while we bit into them. Then we carried on. One incident sticks vividly in my mind. There was one Angolan soldier who was very big, unusually so—he must have been six foot five tall, and weighed twenty stone. He had on his head an old German Army steel helmet, and he was sitting with his back to the cab, and was glaring at us. He took off his helmet to wipe away some sweat just as we were going through some trees, and a low hanging branch hit him on the back of his bare head and split it wide open. The other soldiers in the back just rolled around laughing.

'Anyway, we came to Maquela, which the MPLA had captured, and were taken to the little hospital building. We were helped off the vehicles—we weren't rushed—and were helped along very gently to the hospital. There were a lot of Cubans in there, and one of them said, "Don't be afraid. You're soldiers, and so you're now prisoners of war."

'When they saw the state of me, a doctor was called, and he took a look at me and said something to a medical orderly. He just bent down and shoved a needle straight through my trouser into my leg. I don't know what it was, but I felt a damn sight better later on.'

(Evans and his comrades were allowed several hours' rest before being driven south to an aiport from where, after a two-day delay, they were flown to the capital of Angola, Luanda, and to the Sao Palao prison.)

'*What sort of men were Callan, Copeland, and Christodoulou?*'
'All I can say about them is that they were out and out killers. They deserved to die, all three of them. Callan, you couldn't look at him, Copeland, you couldn't look at him, and Christodoulou was just about the same. They'd as soon shoot you as look at you. You could never trust them. They were just psychopathic killers. They deserved to be killed, every one of them.'

'*According to Dempster and Tomkins, Callan and the others were involved in daily toppings of prisoners, civilians, etc. Can you verify this?*'
'That was certainly not the case while I was out there. He did, as I have said, machine-gun some shacks whose occupants had moved, as he thought, some mines, and I witnessed the killing of the young British mercenary in Maquela, and I was told that an MPLA despatch rider had been killed by having a shotgun thrust into his mouth and then fired, but I reckon that a lot of what has written in Tomkins' and Dempster's book was made up. I know Callan was a bad 'un, but I don't believe that he did half the stuff that they said he did. They have exaggerated a lot. But I must say that Callan was extremely brave—he just did not know fear.'

'*What about the trial? How did you feel about that?*'
'Well, the trial came as a bit of a shock to us. We weren't told about it until we had been in prison about a month or so. They told us it was going to be an international trial with international lawyers, and everything. Right from the start, we didn't expect it to be fair. And it wasn't fair. It was all one-sided. We were represented by mostly Communist or socialist countries, and their type of justice is not like ours. They have no right of appeal like we have. I thought it was a big sham. It was a show trial—that's all it was.'

'*Did you think you were going to be shot?*'
'When we were first in prison, yes. When they didn't tell you a thing, but just come and take you out of your cell and round the back, and interrogate you, of course you think you might be for it. They accused me of telling lies when they knew I wasn't, and on a couple of occasions said that if I didn't tell the truth they'd take me out and shoot me. But I didn't worry too much about, because before long I got the idea that I wouldn't be shot. I became friendly with one of the Cubans, and he told me through a Portuguese who was sharing my cell that he knew that I would eventually go home and that he had seen documents stating this. I would be given a prison sentence, I would not be shot.'

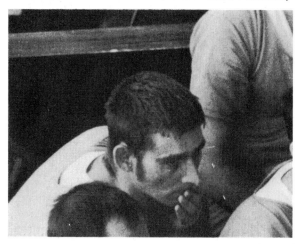

*Evans concentrates in court. 'I thought it was a big sham.' (GAMMA/Spooner).*

*'How did you feel after you were sentenced to 24 years' imprisonment?'*

'When the judge passed sentence on us, I laughed—to myself, not outright. I thought it was ridiculous. I'd been given 24 years, but what the hell for. No one in their right mind wouldn't start handing out sentences like that—16, 24 and 30 years. They gave the death sentence out to four blokes, but only one of them deserved to die, and that was Callan. The other three were murdered, nothing more, nothing less, simply murdered.'

*'How did the men sentenced to be executed react?'*

'I don't think that either we or they thought they would actually be executed. We thought it was a bit of a sham, and that they would be reprieved, but they weren't. Callan by this stage was completely potty. I remember calling out to him one night to shut up. He was shouting out loud as if he was using an army radio, trying to call up somebody in the usual army jargon. Often he used to call out orders, as if he was in charge on the battlefield. By this time he was a proper fruit and nut case.

'One morning they were taken from their cells to a room where they were seen by the ambassador of the time. They were asked to write a letter each to their relatives; they were told they would be shot later that day. Andy McKenzie—the lad with one leg—couldn't write, he was so, so upset. So the ambassador wrote it for him and the ambassador signed it. Later they were taken out to a place outside Luanda called Revolutionary Field, and they were executed there.'

*'What was it like in prison?'*

'There's only one word for that, and that's hell.'

*'What were the conditions and food like?'*

'In the beginning, conditions were extremely bad. When we were first captured, we were each put in an individual cell—one blanket, a sponge, a

*Andrew Mackenzie, 'the lad with one leg',
was so upset, said Evans, that he couldn't
write a last letter home. 'So the Ambassador
wrote it for him, and the Ambassador signed
it.' Then he was taken off to outside Luanda
and shot (Rex Features).*

mattress on the bed, which in my case was dropping to pieces, and no sheets,
pillows, or anything like that. They wouldn't supply those. But what they did
supply us with was bed bugs—the place was literally crawling with them and
there were mosquitoes, rats and cockroaches. After a time you get to like
them, because you spend so much time watching them. As for the food, for
a long time it was absolutely disgusting. It wasn't so bad during the trial
because the Cubans were in charge—they are cleaner than the Angolans, and
they gave us a bit more variety in our diet.

'But the Angolans were mean. I remember looking out of the window and
seeing them bring three pigs. They killed them, cut them up, and ate them,
but the most we got out of them was the pigs' screams. But later on in time,
especially after the attempted coup on 27 May 1977, things did start to get
a little bit better. In time we managed to get the same food as the guards got,
but only because we caused so much trouble. We used to even steal our food.
I got so thin that I was able to get through the bars and into the food store.
But our diet mainly consisted of rice and noodles. There was one occasion,
though, when they gave us macaroni and chicken. It was smashing. We
thought it was our birthday, until we had eaten half the chicken and realized
there was a funny taste about it. The chicken was bad. They had had it so
long that the guards wouldn't eat it, so they gave it to us. We were sick afterwards. The other thing we got was sardines. The Angolans love sardines. But
if you can imagine having that twice a day, week in week out, month in
month out, you'll know we got bloody fed up with it.

'But things got better as time went on. We were eventually allowed
consular access, and were able to buy food. We didn't have cash, or weren't
supposed to. Our families paid in a certain amount each month to the
Foreign Office, and when we had a consular visit we would hand a list in with
things we really wanted. Tea, cigarettes, soap, toothpaste. Also, when we had
cash, we would bribe the guards to go and get us food, such as potatoes,

The mercenary father . . . Colin Evans, of Dewsbury, with his children (left to right): Stephen, Catherine holding Gail and Peter. The picture was taken about four years ago.

THE PARENTS of 26-year-old mercenary soldier, Colin Evans, captured in Angola during the civil war, have given up all hope of their son being represented by a British solicitor.

But they are confident that the Government will send an observer to make sure that he will have at least some defence at his trial on June 8.

On Wednesday afternoon, Mr. David Ginsburg, MP for Dewsbury, heard that the Foreign Office was acting on his suggestion to send an observer from Britain.

"A cable has been sent to the Angolan Government saying we propose to send an observer, who will be in Luanda before the trial," said Mr. Ginsburg.

Mr. Ginsburg said it was not now a question of negotiating whether or not they could send an observer. "It is a definite step forward, the Government has acted positively to my proposal, and have made their position quite clear to the Angolan Government. I hope they will agree to the proposal."

Mrs. Edith Evans said she still felt her son would not be executed. Mr. Clifford Evans, of Walnut Grove, Chickenley, said he was disappointed that there were no public funds to send a solicitor, but was confident everything possible was being done by his own solicitor and by Mr. Ginsburg.

# Better news of jailed mercenary Evans

EIGHTEEN months of uncertainty have ended for the 65-year-old mother of jailed mercenary, Colin Evans, of Chickenley.

Mrs. Edith Evans, of Walnut Drive, received a letter from him — the first in 18 months — saying he was improving after a stay in hospital.

British Embassy officials in Luanda sent the letter to Mrs. Evans after they had visited him in the Angolan jail where he has been a prisoner for nearly five years.

Evans was sentenced to 24 years as a mercenary during the Angolan civil war. Some mercenaries were executed.

News of Evans in recent months has been spasmodic and uncertain, and although prisoners were allowed to write home, Mrs Evans had not heard from her son for 18 months.

"It was wonderful to know that his health is improving and that our parcels are getting through to him," said his mother. "We have been sending him parcels and money nearly every month and it was heartbreaking to discover recently that he had not been receiving them."

Mrs. Evans also received a letter from the Foreign Office describing Colin's condition. Embassy officials said he appeared relaxed and was enjoying his weight-training.

"They have also said I can expect a letter from Colin once a month. For some unexplained reason, Colin's

Mrs. Edith Evans, mother of jailed mercenary, Colin Evans, who has received her first letter in 18 months from Angola.

letters have not been reaching us.

"The Foreign Office have now come to an arrangement with the Angolan Government and Colin's letters will be passed monthly to the British Embassy after vetting by the prison authorities.

"The Embassy are also buying things the prisoners need. But they have asked us to send £15 a month to cover the cost. This is going to be a terrible hardship for me as it already costs me and the family about £15 a month to send Colin a parcel — postage alone is about £9."

*They also suffer who wait at home. Colin Evans' mother underwent years of anxiety back in Yorkshire while waiting and hoping for the safe return of her son. Quite apart from having to see from a distance her son put on trial for his life, she then had to sit and wonder if he would ever be released. News of his condition was hard to come by at first, and when*

# FACING THE FIRING SQUAD

*May 10th 1976*

**THESE are the 10 British mercenaries soon to go on trial in Angola . . . and face the threat of death by firing squad.**

It is the price they could pay for their ill-fated part in the Angolan War.

And as they wait for their trial—due to begin on June 8—the anguish of their families grows.

For since they were arrested three months ago, the new Angolan leaders have refused to let the men send messages home.

## British mercenaries in Angola war trial

By JOHN HILL

## COLONEL CALLAN

### COSTAS GEORGIOU

● HE is foremost among the accused mercenaries, who knew him as "Colonel" Callan.

Georgiou, aged 25, is said to have ordered the deaths of 14 of his men for refusing to fight.

He is also alleged to be responsible for the massacre of 160 African villagers. He was born in Cyprus, but his parents live in London.

The Foreign Office in London said: "We have been trying to get details from the Angolan authorities. But, so far, they have not responded."

### Fainted

**Kevin Marchant**

● HE once served in the Royal Artillery. His wife, from whom he is separated, has said: "He never cared about the money—only the fighting. Marchant, aged 25, comes from Borehamwood, Herts.

But, last night, one mother was giving thanks because, at long last, she knew that her 20-year-old son, John Nammock, was at least alive.

Mrs Noreen Nammock, of Hazelwood Crescent, West London, said: "Through a mix-up over the spelling of his name, I had been unable to discover whether he was really still alive.

"Now, because of details about his date of birth and past from Angola, I know that he is there.

"I nearly fainted when I heard the news. For months I have been ringing every telephone number I can think of where there might be some clue about him.

"He is the elder of my two sons and comes from an army family.

"John is the adventurous kind, whose idea

of life is to be parachuting out of planes.

"I have been taking tranquillisers to help me sleep at night.

"Now I feel 100 times better—even though I am so worried about what will happen to him."

### Caution

The list of Britons to be tried — announced by Angola's Justice Minister Dr Diogenes Boavida — is still being treated with caution by another mercenary's mother.

Mrs Catherine Lawlor,

of Broom Hill Road, Farnborough Hants, said of her son also called John:

"I am 99 per cent sure that he is being held by them but I dare not positively believe it yet.

### Fear

"Then there is the fear of what happens next.

"John is a strong character. — you do not go through Royal Marine training without becoming self-sufficient.

"But I would dearly love to be able to go to Angola for the trial."

**Michael Wileman**

● HIS mother, who has six children, lives in Peckham, London. Wileman, aged 19, was still in council care when he signed up with the mercenaries.

**John Barker**

● He was captured while trying to flee Angola by swimming across the River Zaire. Barker, aged 30, is believed to have lived in Farnborough Hants.

**Colin Evans**

● HE is a father of four, but separated from his wife. Evans, aged 28, is a former regular Army soldier. His father lives in Dewsbury, Yorks.

**Cecil Fortuin**

● HE was born in Cape-town, but brought up in the Midlands. Fortuin, aged 32, was left for dead after being injured in Angola during an enemy advance.

**Malcolm McIntyre**

● His real name is Malcolm Wright. He is aged 27, a father of two, separated from his wife and was unemployed before joining the mercenaries.

**John Nammock**

● HE is an ex-Parachute Regiment soldier who lived in West London. Nammock, aged 20, comes from a family with a long Army connection.

**Andrew McKenzie**

● HE is another ex-Parachute Regiment man and a friend of mercenary Michael Wileman. McKenzie, aged 26, left the paras after six years.

**John Lawlor**

● HE is a former Marine from Farnborough, Hants. Lawlor, aged 23, once did a term of duty in Ulster. Was reported killed in Angola.

## I am ready to die, says Callan

"COLONEL CALLAN," the man who ordered the massacre of 14 British mercenaries, told the five judges at the trial in Luanda yesterday that he was ready to die for his actions during the Angolan civil war.

The Cypriot-born Callan — real name Costas Georgiou—said: "I am not proud of my actions and any sentence you give I am prepared to take.

"More than anything I am afraid of prison. No one wants to die, but I am prepared to die."

### Admits

It was the last day of the trial in which Callan and 12 other mercenaries face a possible death sentence.

In addition to leading the massacre of the men who did not want to fight Callan admits killing an Angolan soldier and a civilian.

The sentences are expected to be announced in the next day or two.

## Mercenary verdicts 'fair'

THE Angolan Justice Minister, Mr. Diogenes Boavida, last night defended the death sentences and long prison terms for 13 mercenaries as a reflection of socialist justice.

"We think what we have in this trial shows the world our greatness and our political maturity despite the youth of our State and our Government," he told a Press conference.

He said he did not know when President Agostinho Neto would reach a decision on the three Britons and one American sentenced to death.

Editorial comment — P.8.

IAIN WALKER calls from Luanda, Angola. The mercenaries on trial here will be sentence publicly at 1.30 p.m. tomorrow.

Anyone sentenced to death will face the ritual of a nightmare dawn walk to a firing squad in a jail courtyard—a flat cigarette, a blindfold, a bare wall and a hail of bullets.

Those who are jailed

will go to a convict ranch, where the official policy of the revolutionary far-Left Government is to "re-educate" wrongdoers instead of punishing them.

They will look after cattle and grow strawberries and pineapples.

And even if they are given long terms, it is unlikely they will serve more than a few years before being expelled back to Britain.

*Colin became ill in prison, it was difficult to find out how ill and what treatment he was receiving. She also kept a scrapbook of press cuttings from those years, part of which is reproduced here.*

onions, and so on, but they were very expensive. So if we got a parcel of clothes from home, we'd sell the things we didn't need.

'Also, after the coup attempt in 1977, I did start working. We were the only people the Angolans could trust. It was us who took the food round the cells, and we worked from six in the morning to about nine at night, carting food, preparing it, cleaning offices. The guards were often lucky to get two or three hours of sleep at night. They were shattered. We would go into rooms, move weapons about, we could have equipped an army with weapons that we shifted, but we never bothered.'

*'You say things were better after 27 May. What exactly happened as far as you were concerned?'*

'There was a large gun battle when the rebels attacked the prison. There were a lot of people killed, including prisoners. When the rebels had taken control of the prison, all the cells were opened. They came and took us mercenaries outside, and put us against a wall, and we thought we had had it. We would have been dead in any minute if it hadn't been for a woman who was in charge of the party attacking the prison. She said, "No. We'll not shoot them now. We'll do it tonight." But a short time afterwards, the attackers left the prison, and shortly after that the Cubans and the Angolans marched in.

'It was two or three days after this that we started to work round the prison, and in time we got even more freedom. I ended up working at a garage. So it became easier for me to get my hands on little luxuries, like a drop of coffee and cheap cigarettes. Later on I became the prison electrician. I can honestly

*The imprisoned mercenaries put on a cheerful front for BBC reporter Brian Barron. But prison, especially in the early days, was anything but fun (BBC).*

'Satch' Fortuin, Evans and John Lawlor look pensive during a 1980 interview with Martin Woolacott (Guardian).

Malcolm McIntyre and (half hidden) John Nammock (Guardian).

say that I put a light in every cell in the prison. In fact I forged signatures, made out invoices, lied my way into getting materials, and I even bartered materials with the guards—electric cable, fluorescent lights, you name it. They saw me all right for food and cigarettes, and I saw them all right for lights. You see, I was in charge, and they couldn't touch the materials without my permission.'

'What about medical treatment?'
   'That was difficult. We had to fight for what we could get. If we were sick,

John Lawlor, Mick Wiseman and Kevin Marchant (Guardian).

only in the later times would we get, eventually, to the hospital. We all spent time there, because the food wasn't good.'

*'How did you get on with the guards?'*
  'We got on great with them. We saw one or two kill themselves because of pressure—maybe because they were not allowed to go and see their families. In general they were a nice set of lads. They used to come to our cells, sit down, have a cup of coffee, tell us their problems. In fact they trusted us, and we helped them if we could. We met one or two of their wives, and I even looked after their children when they went out with their wives for a bit. That was the sort of relationship we had with them.
  'But all this was in the last three or four years. Early on they were frightened of us, and I mean frightened. Their chiefs used to threaten them by saying, "If you don't behave yourselves, you'll get thrown in with the mercenaries". They would have them shaking with fear because of our past reputation. But we wouldn't have harmed them. We only ever helped them.'

*'How did you learn that you were going to be released?'*
  'We first got an idea that we would soon be going home when we were called over to the command building in the prison and were met by four doctors. One was a Cuban bone specialist, one was a surgeon, one was an ordinary GP, and the other I'm not sure. We had to strip off naked, and then were given a full medical examination by each one in turn. This was a really in-depth examination and lasted all afternoon. We asked them what it was all about, but they wouldn't tell us. We had a good idea, though, because they had never done this before. Two or three days later, we were called to the command again, and were told we were going to be issued with a new suit each. We got a suit, shirt, tie, socks and shoes—very nice. We were told that these were for our consular visits, and we were not to wear them otherwise. They must have thought we were stupid, because you don't get stuff like that from them for a consular visit. It's too damn warm to wear a suit out there, anyway, or a tie. You're better off in just a pair of shorts and nothing else. We prodded and prodded, but we still didn't get any information out of them.
  'But one Saturday morning, the chief came up to our cell and said, "Get yourselves ready. You're going to speak to the television." We were convinced then that we were going home, but they wouldn't admit it. So we went and spoke to the television, and they asked how we had been treated. We clicked on straight away; we weren't going to make any adverse comments about our treatment since it wouldn't have benefited us. So we told them we had been looked after OK. We were also asked if we would be grateful to the Angolan people if we were released, and we, of course, said we'd be very grateful. But they still wouldn't admit to us that we were going home.

'About five o'clock, the chief came to us and told us that the next day we would be going for a visit to the new installation, that is to say the new prison that had been built about two miles away. This is almost unique—there are only two like it in the whole world, one in Moscow and one in Cuba. They are Russian-built and designed. So the next day we were driven up to the new installation, and taken into the visitors' room. We knew it was bugged, but that didn't worry us. So we sat and waited, and soon enough the Ambassador came in and the Vice-Consul, and gave us all our mail as he normally did. Then the Ambassador said: "Now, I've got something to tell you. You're flying out tomorrow night."

'Naturally, we were all overwhelmed, overjoyed about this. "But", he said, "There's a condition".

'"What's that?" I said.

'"It's up to you how you play it. The President has agreed to release you on condition that you are to say nothing about it to anyone in the prison. Word is not to be released either here or in England until you're out of the country. If word does get out, the deal will be off, and you won't get home. Now, how would you like your families to be informed?"

'We said we didn't want them to be informed if it was going to jeopardize our release, but we had a talk amongst ourselves and we came up with the solution that our families would be informed four hours after our flight left Luanda. Before we left the Ambassador, he had something else to say, however.

'"You must sign a declaration agreeing to pay back your air fares from Luanda to London."

'We didn't like this. We thought we were being really pressurized. We felt that the government had helped us go out there. In a way, were fighting indirectly for the British government, doing their dirty work. Also the American government who paid us through the CIA. But we had no choice but to sign these forms.

'We told one or two of our close friends that we were going, and the next day, shortly before we left, they let us go round the cells and say our goodbyes. We'd made many, many friends. And when we went to the airport, one or two guards turned up there to see us off. For our flight home, we were to be accompanied by two men—one from National Security, and the other from the Ministry of External Relations—all the way to Paris where they would hand us over to the British consul there. They had plenty of money on them, and they kept sending one of the guards to the bar to buy maybe ten cans of lager at a time, which must have cost them about fifteen dollars a time. But they didn't mind, and we ended up having about eight or nine cans of lager each.'

*'Did you have an uneventful flight home?'*
'Not exactly. About an hour into the flight, we were told that we were

turning back. What had happened was that two of the engines had failed and the nose radar had packed in, so we had to return to Luanda, and then spend an hour circling round the town in order to use up some fuel. The National Security man went and made a few phone calls as soon as we had landed. Meanwhile, a flight for Portugal had been prepared, and the aircraft taxied out to the runway ready to take off, but then turned round and came back. All the passengers got off, we were told to get on, and we took off straight away. Later the security man told us that he had phoned the Minister, who in turn had phoned the President, and he had phoned the director of the airport and told him that if the mercenaries were not out of Luanda within two hours, then he and the airport staff would be put in prison. Not surprisingly, we were off the ground in record time. At about three o'clock in the morning, we heard news of our release being broadcast over the world service on the captain's radio—we were over the Sahara at the time, and the sun was just coming up.

'When we landed at Orly Airport, Paris, the British consul met us. But when we went down the aircraft steps, there was a little black vehicle standing there, and waiting by it were two French gendarmes. They said, "Would you kindly step inside", and we thought "Good God, we're getting locked up again". However, they took us just 150 yards across the tarmac, to a waiting aircraft, which we boarded. The door was shut straight away, for it was a scheduled flight and had been awaiting our arrival.

'On board, there were a lot of Press, as well as BBC and ITV television. We told the stewardess that we didn't want to be hassled, and the captain requested all the passengers to keep their seats. He would not let the Press speak to us, though they tried of course. The captain also sent us a drink each, with his compliments, which was very much appreciated. We were met when we landed by a police escort, which included a senior police officer, and a member of the government—I can't remember his name—and they took us to the VIP lounge. The rest of the lads were reunited with their families. I myself didn't want my family to come that far. A man from the DHSS gave me £10, and also a train warrant, but when he made the warrant out he told me that British Rail was on strike until midnight. I said, "How the hell can I get home then?" He said, "I don't know, mate. I can't help you."

'I spoke to my mate Kevin Marchant, who lives in London, and he said "You're coming with us until tonight". So we went to Boreham Wood, and later that evening we went to the pub with Kevin's brother and his family. By this time I had already phoned my brother-in-law and told him I'd be catching a train as soon as they were running, but I got a real nice surprise in the pub because someone approached me from behind, and put their hands over my eyes. It was my cousin and her husband and son. They had driven all the way down from Yorkshire to collect me, which I thought was damn fine of them.

'When I arrived at my mother's house at about two in the morning, all the family was there, and there were tears all around. That was my homecoming.'

*'When you were in prison in Angola, what contact did you have with people back home?'*

'I received a lot of letters from Betty, who I married after I was released. Roughly one a week from about 1977 right up to the time I came home. She kept me going. Without them letters I don't know what I would have done. In fact, I think that if it hadn't been for Betty I'd have gone over the wall and risked being shot. I also got quite a lot of letters from my mother, and one or two from friends, and even a few from strangers whom I'd never met. The first letter I got was before we had even gone on trial. I have still got that letter to this very day, though I won't reveal what she said—it's too personal for that. But I will admit that I was in tears when I read it.

'Another thing I got from my family was a telegram. I got it during the trial, just before I was due to give evidence myself, and all it said was 'Love from home.' It knocked the stuffing out of me. I was so pleased to know my family was thinking about me, that they still thought enough of me and hadn't condemned me.'

*'Looking back, how do you feel about the whole business?'*

'I can't say I regret doing it, because I don't. It was an experience. I have always been an adventurous type. I don't regret doing it, nor what I did. I did nothing that I should be ashamed of, I never murdered anyone.

'One bad thing that came out of it was that I lost my children. But I gained a wife. She's a lass who kept writing to me, who I knew all my life, who kept me sane, who kept me from doing anything stupid. Without her, I could never have done it. And she's the lass I am married to now.

'There are one or two things that I would like straightened out. At the moment, I am being prosecuted by our government for non-payment of my air fare back from Angola. I honestly don't think I should pay for it. We were classed as prisoners of war, and when have you ever heard of prisoners of war having to pay their own air fares home? I think it's diabolical.

'At the moment, times are very hard. I did hope I could get back driving a lorry, but I knew my HGV licence had lapsed. I mentioned this to our Ambassador while I was still in Angola, and he had contacted London, and had got back to me saying that I wasn't to worry as I would get back everything I was entitled to. But when I had been back in England about a week, or maybe it was two, I went to the Transport offices in Leeds and asked them for my licence. They looked into it, and told me that my five years in which I should have renewed my licence had run out six weeks previously. I could not have my licence. I explained that it had been cleared by our Foreign Office, but they said they didn't care what I had been told, the licence could not be renewed.

'That put me out of a job, out of a trade. I have been bumming around now ever since I came home without a worthwhile job. I have since got married, my wife is having a baby, and it is very difficult to make ends meet. We've got no spare cash, no luxuries, no nothing.

'I will just say one final thing. What I have told you here is the truth. I haven't exaggerated, I haven't told you a lie. I would swear this on my life.'

*'One final question. Do you think the British government did all it could to get you released? I get the impression that you are rather bitter about their role.'*

'I do feel bitter. They could have got us out of that prison a long time before they did, but they just were not that interested. Look at the Americans. They were released from prison eighteen months before us, and they didn't even have any representation in the country. But we had a consul out there, and later on an ambassador. And the attitude of the American authorities was so different. Any high American official who visited Angola made a beeline for the prison to visit the American mercenaries, and they also tried to get them freed. But we got a lot of lies from our embassy, and were let down a lot by them. We just didn't trust them. The one exception was the consul John Tomlinson, a big ex-rugby player who liked a pint. We found we could talk to him like we talked to each other—straight. If we thought he needed a blasting we'd give him one, and if he thought we deserved one he'd give us one. He didn't use fancy words: he'd just come out and swear at us. We respected him for it, and he did his best for us. When he went back to Britain on leave, he arranged a meeting of all the men's families. That's the sort of man he was. But as for the rest of them, they were a load of rubbish. They didn't want to do the job they had been saddled with, and they didn't like it when we gave them a hard time. To be honest, a lot of them just were not bothered. They didn't try to help us.

'They kept written notes of everything we said to them at meetings, and we knew for a fact that they opened our mail. We know because on one occasion I got an envelope addressed to me but with John Nammock's letter inside, and he got his envelope with my letter inside. They were both sealed and were not supposed to have been opened. They had come via the diplomatic bag. By this time the Angolans had stopped attempting to monitor our mail, which came to us direct from the embassy, so British embassy staff must have read our mail before passing it on to us.'

(Shortly after giving this interview, Evans appeared in court because he had refused to pay the cost of his air fare back from Angola. On Evan's request to postpone the hearing until he had prepared his defence, the case was adjourned *sine die*. The Attorney-General, curiously, did not send any representative along to the court. Is the case going to be quietly dropped, lest it cause too much embarrassment? At any rate, Evans expressed great confidence in the barrister and Euro-MP Clive Stanbrook who, he suspects, is able to apply the right pressure in the right places. If the Attorney-General does press his case, it will be an act of remarkable vindictiveness.)

I am fortunate to be able to publish here, as a pictorial supplement to Evans's story, a number of photographs taken illicitly with the camera of one of his fellow mercenaries, Mick Wiseman. Wiseman, Evans and Kevin Marchant became close friends during their long stint in prison, and between them they took these photographs during the latter part of their stay.

Wiseman originally got hold of a camera and a single film by having them smuggled into the prison inside a cake. It took, as Wiseman told me, 'a great deal of planning, timing and nerve' to take the photographs without letting anyone else know. By this time most of the mercenaries were in a communal block, each with their own open cell, so privacy was not always easy to find, and Wiseman admitted that he just didn't trust some of the others.

Looking through the photographs, the first thing to strike me was the extent to which food featured in them: Wiseman proudly displaying two pieces of cooked chicken; a table adorned with an assortment of vegetables and fruit; Evans with a goat ten minutes before it was killed; and various shots of the 'kitchen' in which they prepared food.

Also striking was how thin Evans looked by comparison with the two others. He suffered perhaps more than them from the poor prison diet—rice and boiled fish or sardines with no variation for month after month. Evans was reduced to such a state that in the end he just stopped eating, and it was only when he was given a 'special diet' of bread and condensed milk to supplement his rice and fish that he could bring himself to start eating again. At this stage he weighed about 7 stones, compared to his normal weight of 11-11½ stones.

Although conditions were better towards the end of their almost nine years in captivity, they were never easy, and the prisoners' main preoccupation was always survival. This meant, essentially, obtaining food from whatever source they could, and for that they needed money. Thus, when clothes parcels arrived from home, most of the items would be sold for cash, and in time the mercenaries developed a thriving black market in all sorts of commodities. A visit to hospital was often an opportunity to pick up something which could be sold at a considerable profit back in the prison. There was always the danger of getting caught, but since many guards were happy to buy or exchange alcohol or other items obtained by Wiseman and his fellow prisoners, a blind eye was often turned.

To survive also involved trying to keep busy, trying to occupy oneself so that the situation did not become intolerable. For Wiseman, that meant getting himself physically fit, for which he built himself more than one

*Food became an obsession in prison — the key to survival. These peppers, sweet potatoes, avocado pears, and oranges cost Mick Wiseman the equivalent of £50 (Mick Wiseman).*

*The mercenaries' kitchen in the latter days — 'mod cons' were in short supply (Mick Wiseman).*

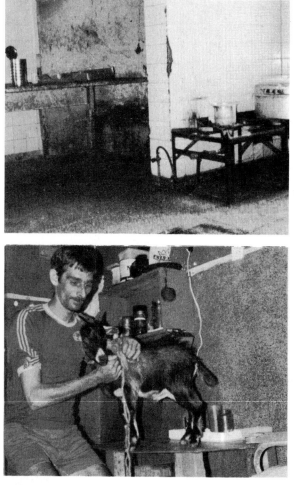

*Evans and a goat which cost him over £150. But it made a very good meal later that day (Mick Wiseman).*

*Kevin Marchant relaxes in his room. The radio was sent from England (Mick Wiseman).*

*Mick Wiseman sits proudly by one of his exercise units. It was later dismantled by the guards, who were suspicious of Wiseman's motives (Mick Wiseman).*

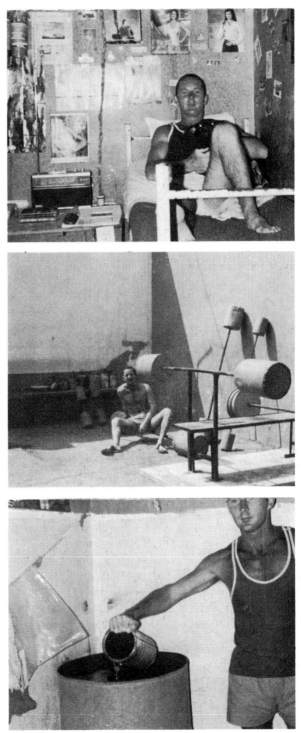

*Kevin Marchant flushes the toilet in the Angolan prison (Mick Wiseman).*

Wiseman writes home. Communication with family and friends helped the mercenaries keep sane, though they knew their letters were all vetted by the authorities (Mick Wiseman).

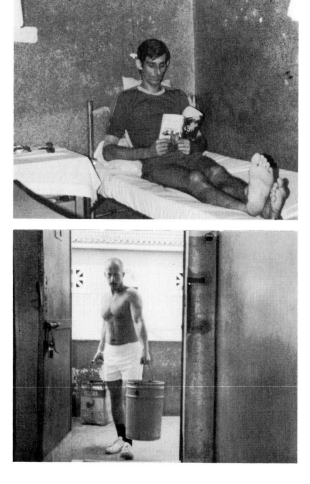

Colin Evans takes it easy on his bed (Mick Wiseman).

Mick Wiseman brings up water for a shower (Mick Wiseman).

*Mick Wiseman displays his supper* (Mick Wiseman).

exercise unit. The guards were highly suspicious, fearing that these efforts to tone himself up were a prelude to an escape attempt, and from time to time the exercise unit would be removed, and soon after Wiseman would start to make another.

He did consider 'going over the wall', but never actually made the attempt, though he told me that he came very close to doing so. But even if he had got out, escaping from Angola itself would have presented much more severe problems.

*Chapter 7*

# Mercenaries for hire—and that's unofficial

'Some jobs the government is involved in. They just want to turn a blind eye.' A mercenary called John.

**Uganda**

The potential of mercenaries for stabilizing or destabilizing a government can be seen very clearly in the recent troubled history of Uganda. In 1979 President Idi Amin's rule of terror was finally brought to an end, much to the relief of the world at large. But hopes that this was to be the beginning of some brave new world, a golden age of peace and prosperity for Uganda, were never fulfilled. President Benaisa took over at the helm, but the goodwill which he initially commanded from the outside world did not lead to any significant economic recovery, and life in Uganda continued to be characterized by lawlessness, corruption and starvation. Consequently, by the end of 1980, Benaisa had himself been overthrown, and replaced by a man who had already held the presidency once—Milton Obote.

At first, Benaisa took up residence in neighbouring Kenya, from where he was able to lend his support to the anti-Obote movement in the continuing game of musical presidents, but this led to him being deported. So from Kenya he moved on to London, where he hoped he would be free to plot and plan unhindered. London has for a long time attracted political refugees and exiles, and for various reasons. For a man like Benaisa there were significant benefits to be derived from being based in the capital of England. One was the fact that by and large it offered him safety from the enemies whom he had inevitably made while President of Uganda. Another was the fact that in London it is remarkably easy to hire professional ex-soldiers.

Bolstered by promises of financial support from 'friends of Uganda' in the West, he approached a recruiter, Mr X, and explained his requirements—namely to regain control of Uganda and keep it. Mr X was in effect asked to arrange and carry out a military coup on Benaisa's behalf. The deal was not, of course, going to be cheap. 'In the initial stages we were talking in the region of nearly £2 million,' said Mr X. When asked what Benaisa's reaction had been to such a figure, he replied: 'He didn't seem surprised at all. He seemed to know that this is what it would take to reinstate him.'

Mr X set about organizing the military details. To ensure success, he reckoned that some 400-500 mercenaries would be required. They would also need to be supplied with weapons. In addition, gunships would be required to provide the speed of movement and air support which Mr X saw as essential to the successful execution of the coup. The operation would be based in Zaire and would be carried out in two stages. The first would involve two groups of mercenaries being airlifted in to attack and take control of Entebbe airport and the centre of Kampala. The gunships would immediately return to Zaire to collect the remainder of the mercenaries and whisk them to the scene of action.

Plans were far advanced when the coup that never was hit a snag.

'We had at that particular time nearly 400 men on call.'

'Ready to go?'

'Ready to go at any time.'

'And plans to get them out of the country?'

'Yes. Yes, that was already in hand as well.'

The snag was that the money which Benaisa was hoping to obtain from his 'friends' failed to materialize. Quite who these friends were he refused to disclose, though, when pressed, he admitted them to be friends in the West rather than in the East. 'What else do you expect? I was on Western soil.' But when these friends—whether individuals or perhaps the CIA—refused to give Benaisa the money for his venture, Mr X aborted the mission and started to look elsewhere for work for his 400 mercenaries.

The connection between Uganda and mercenaries doesn't end here, however. Indeed, the irony is that if Benaisa's coup attempt had taken place, then Mr X's British mercenaries could have found themselves killing—or being killed by—other British soldiers on hire.

Shortly after Milton Obote had taken power, a brochure from a company calling itself Falconstar arrived on the desk of the Ugandan High Commissioner in London. Obote was at this time anxious to improve the internal security within his country. With Benaisa and others active outside the country, and partisans active within, Obote's position was far from secure. He had been deposed from the presidency once before (while attending a Commonwealth conference, always a dangerous time for leaders absent from their countries), and had no desire to let it happen again.

Obote's first impulse had been to approach the British government for assistance, but this, he was told, would not be forthcoming for some time, if at all. It was agreed that a Commonwealth team should provide training for the Ugandan army, but this did not prove entirely successful. When bombing attacks were made on military and police installations, the army responded with counter-strikes, but their heavy-handed methods—involving the arresting, wounding and killing of civilians—provoked the unwelcome criticism of Amnesty International.

The arrival of Falconstar's brochure was, then, very timely. It advertised the company as being one which provided 'manpower and expertise to satisfy the requirements of government for up-to-date advice, training, assistance and equipment supply.' Not that Falconstar was the only such company operating in Britain at the time, but they were more 'respectable' than some. When John Banks had set up Security Advisory Services, he had encountered great difficulty in obtaining work because of unofficial disapproval—'someone in authority was putting the block on us'—but Falconstar seems to have enjoyed the unofficial stamp of approval.

Doubtless this was due to the leadership of the company and the way in which it operated. While Banks was something of a rough diamond, an ex-Para who had been discharged from the Army for driving offences, Peter Lemarchant of Falconstar was altogether a different type. A former Captain in the Scots Guards, he had contacts in the right places and knew how to make use of them. When he was approached to do a job, one of the first things he would do was seek approval from Whitehall.

'We simply ring the desk at the Foreign Office that is concerned with the area of the world that we are talking about. We say we've been asked to do this job and can we come along to talk about it. Obviously, they always say "yes" because they want to know what's going on, and thereafter we take the advice.' Not, it must be added, that Lemarchant is often told to refuse a job. Indeed he admitted to it happening only once when he was told—of a job in the Middle East—'We think you'd be much better employed in doing something else'. The Foreign Office will not, it needs hardly be added, admit to giving any such stamp of approval or disapproval to private military assignments. It claims to give only the same sort of advice to Falconstar as it would give to any British company selling services overseas.

Such public statements may be taken with a large pinch of the proverbial salt, and it was very likely the fact that Lemarchant was persona grata at the Foreign Office that persuaded Uganda's High Commissioner in London that Falconstar was the right company for the job. So, in 1982, Falconstar sent out a group of ex-soldiers to train and organize the Uganda Police Special Force. The role of this 5,000-strong body was not policing in the conventional sense; rather its role was to operate against the guerrillas. Lemarchant compared its activities to those of the British Army in Northern Ireland—'such things as road blocks which prevent movement of terrorists, searches, guarding of vulnerable points'—and providing protection for political figures. Although Falconstar brought considerable expertise to the job, the security measures adopted generally within Uganda continued to cause concern at Amnesty International. In due course the Commonwealth team was withdrawn, and when the British government signed an agreement with Obote to send out a twelve-man team to run Sandhurst-style courses, Falconstar's contract was brought to an end.

**Right** *President Milton Obote of Uganda who hired the 'respectable' Falconstar to train the Uganda Police Special Force (Camera Press).*

**Below** *Troops of the National Liberation Army of Yoweri Museveni, which overthrew Milton Obote (Camera Press).*

General Tito Okello asked Defence Systems to fly missions against Museveni's NLA. They apparently refused, but others did not. Okello was finally piloted to safety by a Canadian (Camera Press).

But again this is not the end of the story, for in 1985 another private military company, Defence Systems Ltd of London, was found to be operating in Uganda. Again it was headed by a man with a fine track record in the British Army—former SAS officer Alastair Morrison. Defence Systems was contracted by Obote to teach Ugandans the low-level tactical flying of helicopters, at a time when his position was growing more and more insecure in the face of increasing guerrilla activity and the decreasing popularity of the regime. Only three weeks after the Defence Systems' team arrived in Uganda, however, the whole situation blew up in their faces as the forces of the next man fated to be Uganda's president, Yoweri Museveni, advanced victoriously on Kampala. This presented Defence Systems with the question of whether to take any active part in resisting the attack on their employer. The official line which they took was that taken by all such companies, that they were only acting as trainers and advisers. Morrison insisted that 'there was no question at all of flying missions', but he did admit that 'the Goverment asked our chaps to fly the helicopters operationally. Of course, we totally refused.' Whether this was truly the case is not clear. Certainly the Defence Systems team, seeing the way things were going, was quick to leave the country, but there is also evidence that some white mercenaries—possibly not British—did fly the helicopters for the government against Museveni's men. And General Tito Okello had a Canadian pilot, Bill Waugh, as his personal 'driver', and was flown to the safety of the Sudan by him.

Ultimately, the truth does not much matter. What the whole episode goes to show, however, is the demand there is for mercenaries—whether companies or individuals—around the globe wherever governments feel insecure and face armed rivals. Also highly typical is the way in which the mercenaries operate with the unofficial blessing of the country from which they derive. Of course, the authorities always disclaim such knowledge— predictably, the British High Commission in Kampala would only admit to being 'loosely aware' (whatever that may mean) of the presence of Defence Systems in Uganda—but the overwhelming evidence is that the British authorities not only are well informed about and give tacit approval to the activities of mercenaries operating from Britain, but also actively assist the mercenaries in the carrying out of their operations—as the rest of this chapter will document.

## The customs dodge

The recruiter Mr X may prefer to keep a lower profile than more 'respectable' outfits like Peter Lemarchant and Falconstar, but that does not mean that his activities are unknown to the authorities. Far from it. Indeed he asserts that when he is approached to do a job, one of the first things he does is to make discreet enquiries from the British security services to see if such a job meets with their unofficial approval.

'If we get a feedback of information which would indicate that they wish us not to proceed, then we drop the whole operation.'

'Always?'

'Always!'

'Even if the money is tempting?'

'Oh yes, yes. We cannot afford to do anything that would embarrass this country.'

But it is not just the case that Mr X wants to avoid embarrassing his country. The fact is that he knows that from time to time he will need the help of the security services. In particular he may need help to get his men back into Britain. When asked what usually happened when his men flew into Heathrow after an assignment, he asserted: 'It's no problem. We get assistance, if need be, from Special Branch. We don't have any problem. It's quite easy to come in.' Sometimes that assistance does not involve more than having someone sympathetic on hand should difficulties arise when coming through customs. ('We didn't actually need assistance, but it was nice to know there were friendly faces, shall we say, if needed.') On other occasions Special Branch gives more active help, such as in assisting them to avoid going through customs control altogether, and so entering 'through the back door'.

Not, of course, that Scotland Yard or any other official source would admit to any such collusion, but there is plenty of evidence to support Mr X's assertions. Take for instance the evidence of a mercenary with several overseas operations under his belt—'John'. He told how, on one occasion, after a five-week job in Africa, he and his colleagues got off the plane at Heathrow to be met by a man who identified himself as being from Special Branch. He showed them to a waiting van and they were then driven off through the cargo entrance of the airport, thus bypassing Customs. Such things he considered to be typical. He was surprised only that people should be surprised that such things go on. For, as Mr X said, 'Everyone knows this mutual assistance goes on'.

Then, too, there is the evidence of the Angola episode. It is no secret that the funding of the mercenary activity there in 1976 came from the American Central Intelligence Agency. The evidence is overwhelming, starting from the evidence of CIA man John Stockwell, and going right down to the mercenaries themselves. Barker revealed how, when he received his initial payment in London, the money consisted of pristine dollar bills. These, he was told, had come from the CIA, and Banks warned him and the others to be sure to mix up the numbers.

If the CIA was so interested in ensuring that the mercenaries were hired in the first place, it is certain that the British security services must have been kept well informed about what was going on. Their hand can be seen in an incident which occurred when the first small batch of mercenaries passed through Heathrow on their way out to Angola. There was a hitch at passport control. McAleese handed over to the officer on duty a sheet of paper with the photographs and personal details of the group. The officer told him it was rubbish. Barker, one of the group, then saw McAleese speak to the officer, who in turn picked up a phone. After a minute-long conversation, he put down the receiver and waved the mercenaries through without further ado.

A week later a second batch of mercenaries numbering nearly a hundred men flew out of Heathrow Airport bound for Angola. Despite the enormous amount of publicity that the recruiting had attracted, and despite the fact that it was now known that one of the first batch, Barker, had jumped bail and had been put on Interpol's wanted list, there was no attempt even to monitor the mercenaries, let alone to hinder or stop them from flying out of Britain. Satch Fortuin, Banks' bodyguard and one of this second draft, admitted: 'There was no passport control. We went straight through the departure lounge and then on to the plane.' When asked if that was a normal procedure, he asserted that Banks had told them: 'Everything is OK. We have help from above. Everything is taken care of.'

Furthermore, the third and final batch of mercenaries also had a straightforward passage through the airport on 8 February. Doubtless they too had 'help from above' for the police present on that occasion, far from checking out the mercenaries, merely made sure that the journalists thronging the airport were kept well away from them.

It was not, however, just a case of the British police and security services

Three recruits for Angola leave Bishopsgate police station after they were detained on suspicion of carrying firearms. Harold Wilson later vehemently attacked the recruiters, but no attempt was made to stop mercenaries leaving Britain — indeed, Banks alleged that he had help from above (Associated Press).

turning a blind eye and allowing the mercenaries through passport control with impunity. John Banks later told the *News of the World* that he had in fact been approached by the Special Branch about his operations. They wanted not only to check out his activities, however, but to include a couple of their own undercover men amongst the recruits. One of these later collapsed and died of a heart attack brought on by the heat, and the other, Banks said, was later wounded in an ambush.

In short, then, the evidence of the connivance and involvement of the British security services in these events is incontrovertible, yet on 10 February, two days after the third batch had flown out, Prime Minister Harold Wilson waxed eloquent in the House of Commons about the men who had recruited mercenaries for Angola. 'Small-time crooks with records have become possessed of vast sums of money, sums far greater than they could ever earn in other ways honestly or dishonestly, and have obtained access to lists of names of former soldiers, SAS and the rest, and signed them up as mercenaries in conditions which I hope the whole House would regard as utterly abhorrent to our system and standards in this country.' If this was indeed the Prime Minister's heart-felt view of the subject, one wonders why he had not attempted to make life more difficult for the mercenaries and their recruiters before this time. The answer, no doubt, is that the mercenary affair in Angola had, by 10 February, suddenly become a hot political potato with the news that Callan had massacred a number of British mercenaries. Hence Wilson's sudden burst of righteous anger. Yet, while Banks and his fellow recruiters were hardly paragons of virtue, to imply, as Wilson did, that it was they who were entirely to blame, and that the government could do nothing to prevent or hinder the hiring and despatching of mercenaries to Angola, was itself dishonest.

Indeed, strictly speaking it was, and still is, an offence under British law to engage in mercenary activity. A nineteenth-century law declares this to be

**Left** *Harold Wilson — 'mercenaries... utterly abhorrent to our system and standards in this country'* (Associated Press).

**Below** *The police get a grip on a mercenary just returned from Angola — but no attempt was made to stop the mercenaries leaving Britain in the first place, though many of them did not have passports* (Camera Press).

the case, but it has long since fallen into disuse, and the Diplock Commission, announced by Wilson on this very occasion, later concluded that it was unworkable. Yet even if it might have been unwise for the government to try and enforce this law, it could easily have made life much more difficult for the recruiters had it so wished. Most notably, the government could have ensured a much more stringent checking of individual mercenaries as they passed through Heathrow. Many of them did not have their own passport, and on that ground alone departure could have at least been delayed. Furthermore, a number of the mercenaries had criminal backgrounds, which ought to have made the police particularly anxious to check them out. The first batch included a well-known safe-breaker, Dave Tomkins, and Barker who was discovered, shortly after he left, to be actually on bail pending a court appearance.

Equally, the second and third batches included men whose main motive, apart from the money, was to escape from the consequences of a criminal offence. Yet the police turned a blind eye—until, that is the manure hit the fan and the backgrounds and activities of the mercenaries became the focus of attention for the world's Press. When the mercenaries began to return to Heathrow, disillusioned, bedraggled and, in some cases, injured, the police suddenly sparked into life, and made some arrests. Thus ex-Guardsman Norman Hollanby was found guilty of a theft committed before he left England, and of breaking the terms of a previous suspended sentence. He received nine months. Dennis O'Brien, who was found guilty of burglary, was sentenced to twelve months.

The ease with which the mercenaries were recruited, and the way in which they were allowed to leave for Angola without any hindrance—indeed, with positive assistance—must have been, as Banks admitted, the consequence of having 'help from above'. Indeed the whole episode stinks of government hypocrisy and official connivance, and merely serves to confirm the more general allegations of the recruiter Mr X, the mercenary John, and Peter Lemarchant, the 'respectable' head of Falconstar: most mercenary activity emanating from Britain is not only known about by the authorities, but is approved by them, and usually the security services are ready and willing to lend the mercenaries their assistance if it should be required.

## Connivance, connivance everywhere

However, Britain is not the only place where such things happen. There is every reason to believe that it happens in many countries. One mercenary based in Britain told me that he had on a couple of occasions worked in France and Spain. He had been recruited by an agency which operates from a European capital. It has no official existence or address, but it exists nevertheless. In each case he was originally sounded out over the phone and he never met the man at the other end of the line. He was unwilling, for obvious reasons, to disclose the details of what the operations involved, but he volunteered that the work was being conducted on behalf of government agencies. That is to say, he was doing jobs which government agencies wanted done, but which they didn't want done by their own operatives. Recommended ex-professionals totally unconnected with them were both reliable and, in the event of something going wrong, much safer for their reputation.

The abortive Seychelles coup (see chapter 3) is a classic example of a well organized mercenary operation being carried out with the connivance of a country's security services. That some members of these services were deeply implicated in the enterprise is certain. The only uncertainty is the question of how far the connivance went. Did top members of the South African government know what was going on? Of course, the Prime Minister

The hiring of mercenaries for both covert and training purposes is as prevalent as ever today, but as well as mercenaries the purchaser also has to procure weapons. Countries are able to buy arms, via reputable dealers, but individuals and unofficial organizations can obtain whatever they need easily enough, too. One recruit described how he could find a dealer in almost any European country he cared to think of who would provide him with whatever weapons he required. Such weapons would cost above the market rate, but there would be no difficulty in getting hold of them. John Banks has said that if he was trying to buy arms, he would go to Spain, Portugal, Yugoslavia and Czechoslovakia because it is comparatively easy to move weapons around in those countries without an end-user's certificate. This is a document which specifies the country to which the arms are bound. If weapons are required for covert military activity, than a false end-user's certificate is required — and it is not, it seems, difficult to bribe diplomats at embassies to authorize such certi-

ficates for bogus destinations. So, the manufacturer gets his sale, the dealer his cut and the mercenaries their weapons.

Shown here are examples of the many weapons, including British, Italian and Israeli sub-machine guns, an SLR rifle and a Bren gun, which are widely available in the arms world (G. Cornish Collection, Beretta SpA, Israel Military Industries, MARS).

*A vast cache of arms seized in Angola* (GAMMA/Spooner).

fervently denied it, but that means nothing. Perhaps more significant is the fact that the South Africans only brought mercenaries to trial as a consequence of international pressure, and that Hoare only served less than four years of a ten-year sentence. The government was without doubt sympathetic to his cause, and it is not hard to believe that leading politicians were informed of what Hoare was planning, and agreed that he should be allowed to continue with his operation in the hope that it would be successful.

There is little reason to doubt that such 'unofficial official' connivance takes place in virtually every country which exports mercenaries. That it takes place in the USA, for instance, where there is even a law against mercenary activity on the statute books, is transparently the case. The Neutrality Act lays down that it is illegal either to recruit mercenaries in the United States of America, or even to plan a mercenary operation from there. In having such a law, the USA is some way ahead of most other countries in the world, yet in practice the law is never enforced. American 'mercs' have long interfered violently in the affairs of Central America, but they are not prosecuted for it.

One man heavily involved in the recruiting of mercenaries is Tom Posey; a former member of the National Guard, he is head of Civilian Military Assistance, an organization which exists for the purpose of sending men to fight against Communists in Central and South America. By and large it is American citizens whom the CMA despatches on anti-Red crusades, though it does on occasion extend its net further afield. Thus in mid-1985 Posey admitted to having put out feelers in Britain where he persuaded some thirty to fifty ex-Servicemen to cross the Atlantic and join the right-wing Contra rebels in their war against the elected, but left-wing Sandinista government of Nicaragua.

Another man active in the same game is the self-styled 'Dr' John, experienced in both organizing and taking part in military operations. He was behind the attempt in 1983 to overthrow the government of Surinam in South America, and has fought alongside the Contras on more than one occasion. In 1984 he attended a convention organized by the *Soldier of Fortune* magazine, and there he saw fellow 'mercs' who had been killed in Nicaragua being publicly honoured. ('I would submit to you, Ladies and Gentlemen,' the assembled company was told, 'that the reason these people died was because they believed. We believe, don't we, Ladies and Gentlemen?')

*Soldier of Fortune* is a magazine which was founded by the doyen of all American anti-Communist mercenaries, Robert K. Brown. Formerly in the US Special Forces, he has fought and 'advised' in Guatemala, El Salvador and Nicaragua, as well as further afield in Afghanistan and Rhodesia. He founded *Soldier of Fortune* to be, as its subtitle declares, 'The Journal of

Professional Adventurers', and he himself is proud of the way it draws attention to areas of anti-Communist conflict where opportunities exist for the 'professional adventurer'. Until recently, the advertisement pages of the magazines have carried many personal adverts from would be 'mercs' looking for paid assignments, and Brown himself is active in sending 'volunteers' to assist in anti-Communist movements in the Americas.

Yet neither Tom Posey, Dr John, nor Brown are prevented from doing what they do, despite the existence of the Neutrality Act. Posey is aware of its provisions, but claims that he does not contravene them. 'I don't hire anybody. These people are volunteers. All we offer is support.' That this 'support' involves rather more than an encouraging pat on the back may be judged from the case of two mercenaries, Peter Glibbery and John Davies, who were 'helped' on the way to Nicaragua by Posey in 1985. They only made it as far as Costa Rica, however, where they were arrested and found to be in possession of arms and money intended for the Contra rebels. Brown takes the same sort of line as Posey. He sends 'trainers' or 'advisers' abroad, nor mercenaries, or 'mercs' as they are generally called in the USA.

Brown also runs mercenary schools, or private, 'military training schools' as he prefers to call them. 'Of course, the schools I manage have never been in the United States: Afghanistan, El Salvador, Nicaragua, Honduras. . .but never the United States.' His training officers are professionals, ex-Servicemen, and the men whom they train are 'members of anti-Communist resistance groups, and soldiers in legally constituted defense forces of non-communist nations'.

Dr John takes specific precautions to avoid the risk of being prosecuted under the terms of the Neutrality Act. The Act forbids recruiting and the planning of mercenary activity in the USA, so 'if I meet a client and we discuss general terms, the situation, and if my investigation proves that it is valid, then we're ready to move into the planning stage, and we go to a foreign country to continue our business'.

Although all three men are based in the USA and their activities can hardly be unknown to the authorities, they are neither prosecuted nor dis-couraged in what they do. On 6 September 1984 President Reagan's National Security Advisor, Robert McFarlane, stated: 'We do not condone and encourage, endorse nor facilitate this kind of thing'. He admitted that it did happen, but insisted that it was not with the encouragement of the United States government. But such statements are unconvincing. Dr John says that the operations in which he gets involved are always in the USA's best interests—by which he presumably means they are always against left-wing/Communist regimes. He also says that US government officials always know where he is working. Indeed, he affirms that 'there have been times when I've had intimate contact with employees of the United States government'. On funding, he is wary of acknowledging his sources, but the implications of what he says are that money sometimes derives from the CIA.

That this should be the case is only to be expected. The involvement of that organization in providing American dollars to hire British mercenaries for Angola is undeniable (see chapter 2), and their involvement in supporting the Contras against the left-wing Sandinista government of Nicaragua is equally apparent. This came most dramatically to the fore in 1984 when it was revealed that a CIA employee—pseudonymously called John Fitzpatrick, a veteran of Korea and Vietnam—had written a ninety-page manual entitled *Psychological Operations in Guerrilla Warfare*. He wrote this as a handbook for the Contras, and in it he advised that they kidnap and 'neutralize' Nicaraguan government officials. In a section entitled 'Selective Use of Violence', the document states: 'It is possible to neutralize carefully selected and planned targets such as court judges, police and state security officials'.

Much controversy arose over such advice and over the meaning of the word 'neutralize'. It was generally interpreted as being a euphemism for assassinate. President Reagan denied this, and when he was asked to explain what it did signify, he told reporters at a briefing: 'You just say to the fellow who's sitting there in the office, "You're not in the office any more".' This remarkable explanation not surprisingly caused considerable comment. One New York journalist, Anthony Lewis, who was not present, pondered in his column whether any of the reporters present had had the rudeness to express their feelings by laughing out loud. In this situation, the Inspector-General of the CIA realized that something had to be done—or at least seen to be done—and he led an inquiry which came up with the recommendation that a few officials be disciplined. This finding was described by Senator Daniel Patrick Moynihan, Vice-President of the Senate Select Committee on Intelligence as 'appalling'. He said: 'It looks like seven Sergeants are going to lose weekend privileges for a month.'

But the affair only underlines the way in which the Reagan administration has been willing to give its utmost support to the Contras, and to whoever assists or joins them, even if such persons were contravening the laws. As Lewis said, 'The Contras have been carrying out murders and kidnappings for a long time now, and it is no secret that they were financed, trained and organized by the CIA'.

The affair—and the revelation that CIA operatives had planted mines in Nicaraguan harbours in 1984—had the practical consequence of causing Congress to cut off CIA funds and to refuse Reagan's call in 1985 for funds for 'humanitarian aid' for the Contras. By the middle of 1986, however, the pendulum had swung towards the President, and Congress approved a request from him for $100 million for the Contras, of which seventy per cent was earmarked for military assistance. However, the Bill had still not been ratified when, even as this book was in the final process of being written, another incident occurred in Nicaragua which typifies what has been going on in that country. On 5 October 1986 a C-135 transport plane was shot down by a ground-launched missile fired by Sandinista troops in southern Nicaragua, and crashed a few miles north of the Costa Rica border. Of the four-man crew, three were killed, but one managed to bale out to safety. Twenty-four hours later, he was captured, and instantly became a prize exhibit and pawn in the propaganda game. He was identified as an American citizen, one Eugene Hasenfus from Marinette in the state of Wisconsin. Considerable quantities of arms were apparently found in the vicinity of the wrecked aircraft. The official Sandinista communiqué spoke of 50,000 rounds of ammunition suitable for the AK-47 rifles carried by the Contras (and also the Sandinistas as it happens), 'dozens of rifles', grenades and other sundry equipment. Though the details may perhaps be somewhat suspect, it is clear that the plane was indeed carrying arms and ammunition, and that these were intended for the Contras.

Hasenfus was the first American citizen to be captured by the Sandinistas in their war against the Contras, and the incident sparked a predictable outbreak of claims, counterclaims and denials. The Sandinistas claimed that Hasenfus was working for the CIA, and also that he was a military advisor in El Salvador and had been assisting the government against left-wing guerrillas there. The Americans denied this, and stressed that Hasenfus and his dead colleagues were private individuals, not sponsored by the US authorities. Thus George Schultz, the US Secretary of State, stated: 'The people were not from our military, nor from any US government agency, the CIA included. So these are private citizens and it is not a governmental operation.' Similarly Alberto Fernandez, a US Embassy spokesman in Managua, insisted: 'Neither the plane nor the crew had any affiliation with the US government. Neither the plane, the crew, nor the cargo were financed by the US government. Allegations that the individual supposedly held by the Sandinistas is a US advisor in El Salvador are false.'

However, more information about Hasenfus and his dead colleagues was soon forthcoming, at first casting severe doubts upon the official American denials, then completely torpedoing them. Hasenfus was a former US Marine, a veteran of Vietnam. According to the Sandinistas, identity cards were found on both him and the dead pilot; these were signed by General Juan Rafael Bustillo, commander of the El Salvadorean air force, and also revealed that they belonged to a unit called 'Group: USA' air force, and held positions as 'advisers' at the Ilopango Air Base in El Salvador. Furthermore, the co-pilot of the plane, William J. Cooper, was found with a card bearing the name of P. J. Buechler, the operations co-ordinator for the Office for Humanitarian Assistance of the US State Department. This had been established in 1985 to channel $28 million of 'humanitarian aid' which Congress had approved for the Contras. He was also named as a pilot of the Southern Air Transport Company, a private company which one

Congressman, Henry Gonzalez, immediately described as a front for the CIA.

The claims of the Sandinistas were underlined by Hasenfus himself at a news conference on 9 October. He admitted to receiving $3,000 per month to drop arms and ammunition for the Contras, and said he had taken part in a total of ten flights, six from Ilopango and four from the Agucate air base in Honduras. Furthermore, and most damagingly for the official US line, he told reporters that it was CIA men based in El Salvador who 'did most of the organization for these flights'.

Inevitably, Hasenfus was put on trial, and equally inevitably he was, after a 26-day trial found guilty—on charges of terrorism, conspiracy and threatening Nicaraguan security. Since Hasenfus had been caught red-handed, his lawyers concentrated on trying to prove that he had no command responsibility, but the court was not impressed by the idea that Hasenfus was unaware of the nature of the supplies he was flying to the Contras. The three judges concluded that 'there is not the least doubt that the accused carried out this work with the complete understanding of what he was doing'. When the Justice Minister was asked if there was any possibility of Hasenfus receiving a pardon, he denied it. 'What would we get out of a pardon?' he asked. 'If they would tell me that they would stop all aid to the Contras, I would say give them anyone they want, but that is not

*The name of the game is simple — if you capture a mercenary, parade him before the media; if you employ one, you don't even admit it* (The Photo Source).

going to happen.' However, this hard line was not shared by President Daniel Ortega, who immediately admitted that it was unlikely that Hasenfus would remain a prisoner for thirty years. It nevertheless came as a real surprise when, shortly afterwards, just ten weeks after the American had been captured, he was released and allowed out of Nicaragua. The war, however, continues.

It seems certain, then, that Hasenfus was one of the large band of 'private' individuals who have for some considerable time been 'assisting' the Contras against the Sandinistas. They may be 'private' in the sense that they are not officially sponsored by the US government, but there is no doubt that Hasenfus and his dead colleagues were unofficially supported by the CIA. Furthermore, it is significant that, amidst all the denials, there was no suggestion from the Reagan administration that the Neutrality Act should be enforced to prevent private operations like this one continuing.

Just as it has been one of Reagan's most fervent wishes to obtain more financial aid for the Contras in their often vicious war against the Sandinistas, so it has been unofficial policy to support any individuals who have fought for the Contras, or who have sought to recruit 'volunteers' for the cause. For Congressman Jim Leach it is a constitutional conflict: 'When you have private citizens taking war-making authority into their own hands, and when you have a government assist these private citizens, you have a real breakdown in the contract under our constitution between the executive and the legislature. It's this constitutional issue that overwhelms all others by comparison.' Which is another way of saying that despite the provisions of the Neutrality Act, mercenary activity receives not only a Nelsonian turning of the blind eye, but also active assistance from the CIA and other undercover personnel.

## Chapter 8

# Will the mercenary become extinct?

Will mercenaries, like the poor, always be with us, or will they, like the dinosaur and the dodo, one day disappear totally and irrevocably from the face of the earth? It is a question which subdivides into three more. Will there always be a supply of suitable mercenary material? Will there always be a demand for this supply? And will mercenarism ever become a criminal offence, the prevention and apprehension of which will be internationally enforced?

Mercenaries are, almost exclusively, ex-professional soldiers. The recruits who went to Angola included a few who were not, but they were exceptions who proved the rule. Tomkins was a professional safebreaker with no military background who owed his presence amongst the mercenaries to his friendship with Banks. He in the event proved useful in Angola, where his skill with explosives made him valuable to Callan, but others who went out there with little or no military experience quickly found that they were out of their depth. When they refused to go into action, they instantly became a liability, and when they later panicked and shot at their own comrades, this led directly to their deaths. Thus, one thing the Angola fiasco demonstrated most forcibly was that war is not a game for the uninitiated, and that the mercenary life is something for hardened professionals, not for those whose main qualification is a desire to make a fast buck. Hoare too had discovered when looking for recruits that a high proportion of those attracted by advertisements offering money and adventure were totally unsuitable, and at the beginning of each of his three Congo campaigns the first thing he did when a batch of recruits arrived was to weed out anything up to half of them and pack them back whence they had come.

Employers, who have to pay out considerable amounts of money for mercenaries, naturally require men with a good military background, men with both the training and aptitude for fighting. In particular they want men who have served in one of the elite fighting units of the world such as the Parachute Regiment, the SAS or the US Marines, men who can be expected to do the job properly.

To a considerable degree, people become what they do, and this is as true of the army as of any job or profession. An army is, by its very nature, tradi-

There are many crack fighting units around the world; their members are the toughest soldiers, but the toughest soldiers do not make the best civilians when, for one reason or another, they leave the regiments. As one ex-Para told me, 'most of the regiment are cowboys'. For these independent, adventurous types, mercenary service is the obvious option.

**Above** *SAS members undergoing instruction* (MARS).

**Right** *A fully-equipped SAS member ready for a parachute jump* (Irvin Parachutes via MARS).

**Below** *Members of the 1st Parachute Regiment practise with a mortar* (Crown Copyright MARS).

**Above** *A SEAL (member of a Sea-Air-Land warfare unit) swims ashore* (US Navy via MARS).

**Below** *A member of CIDG tests a machine gun at Bu Prang, Vietnam* (USAPA via MARS).

tional and conservative. It expects, indeed demands, that its members conform. Equally it requires of each man a variety of qualities which include obedience, self-discipline and a willingess and ability to kill. To kill is part of the job. This is true for all soldiers, but most especially of the elite units of the world—the Parachute Regiment and the SAS in Britain, the US Marines, the Régiment Etrangère de Parachutistes of the French Foreign Legion, and so on. The qualities valued in the rarefied atmosphere of such units are not the same as those most valued in the civilian world. The intensive training to which soldiers of these units are subjected is intended to make them, as far as is possible, perfect fighting machines, able to survive and operate in the most difficult conditions, and to kill—if not without thought, then at least without feeling. Those who thrive in such a climate are necessarily of an independent, adventurous spirit, who thrive on the fuel of danger and action. As one ex-Para put it, 'most of the regiment are cowboys.'

But what happens to such men when they come out of the Army? For sooner or later, they do come out, and not a few of them do so long before they reach pensionable age. The reasons for these early departures are twofold. The first is boredom. As the role of the British Army in world affairs has diminished, so has the opportunity for active operations reduced. This means that the scope for the elites to do for real the things for which they are trained has been reduced. Banks recalls that in 1969, the year in which he left the Parachute Regiment, a lot of others did too, essentially because they were bored with the lack of action. Others stayed on only because they were given the opportunity to serve on loan in the forces of the Sultan of Oman, who was engaged in the particularly hazardous Dhofar War. But the other reason for an early departure is the one that in fact applied to Banks, and to a number of other men who later served in Angola, including Callan, Hall, Wainhouse and Dempster. They were all dishonourably discharged from the Army for criminal or military offences.

These two reasons—boredom and dishonourable discharge—ensure that there are always available in the outside world a group of highly trained ex-professional soldiers who are temperamentally unsuited to a humdrum civilian life. They leave the Army and very often find themselves unable to settle into a 'steady' job. Their military training has in any case not prepared them for many types of work—ex-soldiers all too often are offered the inevitable choice of working on a building site or collecting the dole. If, therefore, someone offers them good money for doing what they like and do best—soldiering—then they naturally tend to jump at the opportunity.

If the supply of would-be mercenaries is unlikely to dry up as long as nations have professional armies, it is equally true that demand is unlikely to cease unless war itself ceases. As long as there are wars to fight, there will be those who are prepared to pay others to fight for them. This has always been the case, and is as true now as it has ever been.

*Wherever there is violence in the world, there are opportunities for mercenaries and 'volunteers', such as these French soldiers in war-torn Beirut (Rex Features).*

In the foreseeable future, the only way in which demand is likely to be stopped is artificially, that is to say by governments of the world uniting and establishing in international law that mercenarism is a criminal offence. But the evidence suggests very strongly that this will not happen.

In some countries, mercenarism is strictly speaking already a crime. If the Neutrality Act in the United States of America and the Foreign Enlistment Act in Britain were enforced to the letter of the law, mercenaries would be unable to operate from these countries. But, of course, they do. After the Angola fiasco, the Diplock Commission was set up to investigate the situation in Britain, but it concluded that the Foreign Enlistment Act was unworkable. It found that when it comes to banning mercenaries the problems start with the fact that the term 'mercenary' comprises such a wide range of persons. The hired soldier who fights in an army, or for a cause, other than that of his own country can be driven to do so by a whole variety of motives, and it is very difficult indeed to clinically differentiate between a volunteer driven essentially by idealism, and a professional freelance soldier doing what he knows best. The commission decided therefore that a mercenary can only be defined by what he does, not by why he does it. However, the commission also found that to enforce control over the enlistment of such men in foreign forces was a 'restriction upon the freedom of the individual which, in our view, requires to be justified on grounds of public interest'. Further, they determined that 'the use of prerogative power to withhold or withdraw passports. . .is both ineffective and unjustifiable'. Furthermore, they concluded that in any future legislation 'enlistment as a mercenary by a United Kingdom citizen should cease to be a criminal offence and service as a mercenary abroad should not be made one'. The only positive recommendation of importance made by the commission was that future legislation should aim to 'prohibit recruitment in the United Kingdom of mercenaries for service in specified and armed forces abroad', and in particular to prevent the publication of details of such employment in newspapers.

Since the publication of the Diplock Commission's report in August 1976, however, no further action has been taken to try and limit mercenary activity from Britain. Indeed, Britain continues to be one of the main centres in the world for the recruitment of mercenaries.

In 1982 there was an attempt to draft an international convention against the 'recruitment, use, financing, and training of mercenaries'. It included some fine phrases, such as 'recognizing that the activities of mercenaries are contrary to fundamental principles of international law, such as non-interference in the internal affairs of states, territorial integrity and independence, and seriously impede the process of self-determination of peoples struggling against colonialism, racism and apartheid, and all forms of foreign domination,' and 'bearing in mind the pernicious impact that the activities of mercenaries have on international peace and security', but it brought the international outlawing of mercenarism not one iota closer. The insurmountable problem, as the Diplock Commission had already discovered, was that of definition. How do you differentiate in law between an 'official adviser', an idealistic 'freedom fighter' and a freelance professional? The United Nations proposal tried to solve this problem by a more specialized description of the mercenary: 'a specially recruited person that takes part in an armed conflict for private gain and is neither a national or a member of the regular armed forces of any party of the conflict'. But even this leaves loopholes. The phrase 'for private gain' would be seized upon by any lawyer, and does such a definition allow any differentiation to be made between the Cuban 'advisers' who fought alongside the MPLA forces in Angola, and the British and other mercenaries who fought for the FNLA forces of Holden Roberto?

But it is not just the matter of definition which prevents the formation of an effective law banning mercenaries either in Britain or in the world at large. It is also the simple matter of political will. It should be apparent from the rest of this book that mercenaries by and large operate with the knowledge and active connivance of the intelligence services of the countries in which they are based—whether that country is Britain, the United States of

America, France, South Africa, or wherever. While the authorities are loath to admit this connivance, it is, as far as mercenaries are concerned, an open secret. As the anonymous recruiter Mr X said, 'everyone knows this mutual assistance goes on'.

World politics is a field in which morality is all too often allowed no place. As ex-President Binaisa of Uganda said after trying unsuccessfully to hire mercenaries to carry out a coup to return him to power, 'the rules of the game. . .today have grown to such an extent that whoever wins calls the tune. Whoever wins. It is a question of strength. If you win, you call the tune. So everyone recognizes. . .that might is right.' The same amoral view of the matter is expressed by the mercenaries themselves and the recruiters. 'If a country or an individual has a need for a particular service. . .I would provide that service. It's like a gentleman overseas needing a mechanic for his car.'

This is a view shared too by the intelligence services and the men in power in countries throughout the West. Mercenaries are, for them, a very convenient tool of foreign policy. The jobs for which they are recruited are usually anti-Communist and so are generally acceptable to Western governments. If they are not they can be stopped. Mercenary recruiters claim that they keep in touch with the secret services, and say that they are willing to back out of operations if they are asked to do so. And John Banks had considerable difficulty in getting work before the Angola business because he found that clients were being warned off him by 'someone in authority'.

It is, then, very hard to see Western governments ever agreeing to and enforcing a ban of mercenaries. They are far too useful for that. In an age when colonialism is a dirty word, and when Russians and Cubans send out 'official advisers' to further their foreign policies, mercenaries are a very useful tool. They reach, as it were, parts that conventional troops cannot. And, if a mercenary operation goes embarrassingly wrong, it can be totally disowned. In such a situation, it is the mercenaries themselves who are bound to shoulder the blame and, if expedient, to suffer prosecution. It may be hypocritical, but then hypocrisy is hardly a new feature of politics.

Mercenaries are a product of a world which believes in the efficacy of force. They are much in demand. They are here to stay.

# Index